My Baby's Mind

Your mind is a great castle with many wings and many floors.

Throughout your estate you will find many doors.

Behind these doors rooms are spacious and rare,

Vast study halls and libraries with their shelves yet bare.

Secret passages and tunnels now spread all about.

You house grand ballrooms within and terraces without.

Your mind has hidden gardens and wide open parks.

There are paths well lighted and those that are dark.

You have densely-treed woods and grounds with no bounds.

You own great modern cities and quaint little towns.

I, too, once had such a world in my mind.

But people built walls that were too big to climb.

How will I manage to not block your way?

I must find the answer and let you be what you may!

This program is dedicated to my husband Kory, whose support and sincere belief in me made this program a reality, and to our son Jayme, whose coming made us aware of the need for this program.

Enriching the Lives of Children from Birth to Age Two

written by
Lilah LeBouef

illustrated by
Luke Cakalic

BABY E.D., INC.
Baton Rouge, Louisiana

Published by Baby E.D., Inc.
PMB 364, 8733 Siegen Lane
Baton Rouge, Louisiana 70810-1945

Printed in the United States of America.

Library of Congress Cataloging-in-Publication Data
LeBouef, Lilah Townsend.
Baby e.d. the enriched development program: enriching the lives of children from birth to age two / by Lilah LeBouef.
208 pages.
Includes bibliographical references, index, and activities calendar.
ISBN 0-9670253-0-3
1. Developmental Psychology — Infant Psychology
2. Early childhood education
3. Infants — Development
4. Child Development
5. Child Rearing
6. Parenting
BF719.L43 1999 155.422 99-90120
CIP

Cover photograph by Shugart Studios, Baton Rouge, Louisiana.

For the sake of grammatical convenience, he and she are used interchangeably throughout this document to refer to infants, babies, and toddlers of either sex.

Foreword

Babies experience the most rapid intellectual growth during the first three years of life. Many people believe that a child's capacity to learn is based entirely on heredity. However, the facts show that parental involvement in a child's life and learning dramatically affects the child's future. *You* make a difference in what your child can achieve. Increased technology and scientific research has revealed much in this regard. We now know that a child may never be capable of certain types of learning or that some learning may be stunted if he is not exposed to specific stimuli at the appropriate stage of development.[1] Therefore, the findings of these studies are vital to the intellectual development of all infants and toddlers. Much of the research confirms what many experienced parents already knew to be important, and other research reveals the significance of practices which may have otherwise been overlooked. So what exactly should you as a parent or concerned caregiver do to benefit from these findings?

Although volumes have been written to report the findings, practical suggestions for enriching children's lives in the first two years can be difficult to find. This program has been compiled from the latest scientific research as a concise resource for concerned parents, educators, and caregivers. Rather than trying to create a SuperBaby who can perform advanced tricks at an early age, this program is designed to help parents provide an enriching environment for their child's intellectual growth from birth to age two. Rather than trying to "teach" infants by cramming facts or dictating information for rote memorization, it endeavors to "always respect and conform to the natural, spontaneous way children form knowledge."[2] Implementing this program for enriched development can benefit every child, regardless of culture, heredity, and natural mental ability.

Table of Contents

Section **Page**

How to Use This Program

In enriching your baby's development, you must keep several concepts in mind. Infants learn through their bodies, which means that intellectual development is achieved through motor and sensory skill development. Motor skills involve the use of body parts, such as fingers, hands, arms, toes, feet, and legs. Sensory skills, as you might imagine, involve the use of taste, smell, sight, sound, and touch. Since babies do not come pre-programmed with their parents' language, they must use motor and sensory skills to gather information.

Your baby cannot be forced to acquire motor or sensory skills before his body can handle them, but stage-appropriate enrichment can improve his mastery of the skill. This in turn leads to improved intellectual development. However, each child develops at his own pace. Your goal is not to rush his development, but merely to enrich it and thereby afford him every opportunity to reach his full potential. Babies who are loved and encouraged will be on the right track for reaching that potential.

Speaking of not pushing, what should you expect of yourself? Just as you will avoid pushing your baby to be a SuperBaby, you should avoid pushing yourself to be a SuperParent. Expecting too much of yourself can make you a wonderful committed parent one day and an overwhelmed nightmare the next. Your poor baby would never know what to expect. Because he lacks experience and does not yet know that not everything is about him, he would be inclined to believe the changes were a result of his behavior. So be informed and then relax. Your baby's greatest need, a happy, stable, and loving home environment, does not depend on mistake-free parenting.

Part I of this program addresses your baby's *overall development* without regard to age. The chapters provide information, instructions, and studies on how to enrich your baby's development from birth on. Read Part I to discover how your baby learns and what you can do to make his developmental path a smooth one. (See Appendix A.)

Part II of this program addresses the growth of your baby in *six developmental stages*. The stages are grouped according to age for the sake of providing a common measurement. Please keep in mind that the time estimates are just that, estimates of when your child should be ready for the type of stimulation described. Your own little expert will tell you whether he is ready. Your job is to recognize and be aware of his signals.

ROLL, SIT, AND CRAWL

At a birth class reunion, three couples witnessed how differently children progress. The three babies were within three weeks of six months old. Chase (the largest baby) could sit and crawl but could not roll over by himself. Ben Tyler could sit and roll over but could not crawl. Jayme (the smallest) could roll over and crawl but could not sit up by himself. Which baby was the most advanced? All three were doing great!

MEASURING MILESTONES[3]

Many people generally expect a baby to sit up at six months of age, babble "ma-ma" or "da-da" by nine months of age, and walk by their first birthday. Acquiring these skills before or after those markers is then labeled "early" or "late." In light of what scientists have discovered about how babies develop, these labels can be misleading and inaccurate.

The range at which babies begin walking, for example, is wide (between nine months and eighteen months) because there are many variables than contribute to each baby's development: genetics, body build, temperament, muscle tone, and sensory and motor skill development, to name a few.

If you fear there is something wrong with your baby, however, you should trust your instincts and consult with his health care provider right away. If you are right, early detection can be crucial to effective intervention.

If there is nothing wrong, your fears will be laid to rest quickly, and you can get back to enjoying your baby.

Although it is natural for you to care about whether your child is mature or immature for his age, expecting to fit your child into a standard measurement can have a negative impact on your relationship with him. Studies have shown that a child who learns to walk at 13 months of age is not necessarily less intelligent, less motivated, or less of anything than a child who learns to walk at 9 months of age.[4] That child may be perfectly on schedule for his personal development. You have reason to celebrate his new accomplishment, rather than worrying that he should have reached this point months ago.

This does not mean that you should not care about when your child reaches developmental milestones. In fact, your child's health care provider will likely ask about developmental milestones during regularly scheduled checkups. This enables him or her to detect possible health problems. For example, if your child does not start to babble by a certain age, a hearing test may be suggested; if your child does not seem to recognize your face by a certain age, a vision test might be appropriate; and so on. Such monitoring of developmental milestones by parents and health care providers is important. The American Academy of Pediatrics (AAP) website includes a set of guidelines for parents, which is included as Appendix B for your convenience. As stated by the AAP, if your child has not reached these milestones by the age indicated, be sure to bring this to the attention of his health care provider.[5]

Each stage is built upon, rather than replaced. Suggestions made for the first month of life are still valuable in the second month. Information for the third month is merely an addition to what was used in the second month, and so forth. In all cases, your baby's physical and emotional safety should be of primary concern. Where there is room for creativity on your part, always be conscious of your child's physical limitations. For example, although your one-month-old may be ready for an item intellectually, small parts or sharp edges may pose a threat to him physically.

YOUR BABY'S DAY

If you want your baby to be an active learner throughout his entire life, you must set the example. He needs to see you getting excited about learning, being curious and enthusiastic, trying new things. Educational play is just one part of your baby's intellectual stimulation. Besides proper medical care when needed, your baby's day should include the following things:

- Being talked to throughout the day
- Being read to according to his attention span and interest
- Being massaged at least 15 minutes per day
- Listening to music two or three hours per day
- Listening to foreign language(s) at least 15 minutes per day
- Enjoying at least 15 minutes per day of personal playtime with you and no toys

- Getting adequate sleep
- Receiving proper nutrition
- Receiving proper physical care with regard to hygiene
- Receiving unconditional love, support, and affection
- Enjoying loving parental guidance.
- Enjoying a safe, fun environment in which exploration and discovery are encouraged
- Enjoying educational play throughout the day

ALL WORK AND NO PLAY

Every experience can be a learning experience, but that does not mean it has to be. I know a pre-school teacher with three very intelligent children. Her children could read in their toddler years, play the piano and violin since their pre-school years, and have been very advanced in nearly every accomplishment. Their parents love them and take every opportunity to teach them. Sounds wonderful, right? There's one problem: I rarely ever see the children smile. The children are very mature for their age, but they never seem to be having fun. You can make your child's early years really special by keeping learning fun. Raise a happy child!

Every experience during the day can be a positive learning experience. As you go through your daily routine, ask your baby thought-provoking questions and discuss them with him. Why is the sky blue? Why do leaves fall? Where does rain come from? Let your baby see you learning: reading a manual as you assemble something new, reading a book, listening to a new piece of music. Let your enthusiasm shine through for your baby to see in your voice, gestures, and expressions.

GENERAL INSTRUCTIONS

Your baby learns by experiencing an object and acting on it with his senses. He must be the one to initiate this activity. This puts certain restrictions on you as a parent. For example, you would never try to hurry your baby's development by training him to perform certain tricks or tasks. Similarly, you would avoid the temptation of having your baby demonstrate his latest accomplishment for every new visitor that happened along.

Because your baby must initiate his learning, be careful that you play *with* him, rather than *for* him. Simply present him with opportunities to initiate learning. During your child's first few months, for example, before he can crawl, put colorful objects where he can see them. Use interesting objects of different shapes and sizes and textures. One of the objects is bound to catch his attention and make him curious enough to investigate.

Work in harmony with your baby's natural desire to expand his knowledge of the world around him. Infants expand their knowledge by relating new information to what they already know. Maybe your son has been playing with plastic blocks. He knows they are square, can be different colors, and are fairly light. When you introduce wooden blocks, he compares them to the plastic blocks he already recognizes. The wooden blocks are square but heavier, and can have more than one color on the same block. For that matter, they feel different than the soft cloth used to wipe his chin, and they taste different than the drink that fills his belly. Besides that, both sets of blocks are shaped differently from the plastic rings he just held. Now this does not mean your three-month-old can tell the difference between a square and a circle. If you ask him to touch only the wooden blocks and not the plastic blocks, he is likely to just look at you with his usual interest in the sound of your voice. But his brand new computer (his brain) is gradually entering more and more information into his database.

ELEMENTARY, MY DEAR WATSON

Your child is the great Sherlock Holmes, trying to unravel the mysteries of the world around him. You are his faithful assistant, Mr. Watson. You do not investigate directly, but you do most of the legwork. You make sure Sherlock has everything he needs, so that he can stay focused on the mystery at hand. Your baby sees something interesting at the end of her leg. She tries to reach it, but the activity tray of her swing blocks the way. You, good sidekick, put her on her back on a blanket and immediately she grabs that red sock. She pulls it to her mouth but cannot quite taste it. You slip it off her foot and now she knows just what that thing at the end of her leg tastes like!

The relating of information takes time. Only through use and application of your child's newly acquired knowledge can he retain it. Therefore, once he discovers something new, 1) let him explore it fully, and 2) let him repeat it continually until he is ready to move on to something new.

Activities suggested in this manual and on the activities calendar are for your convenience and inspiration. If your baby seems disinterested in the activity you introduce, try something else that does interest him. Repetition, though tedious to adults, is vital to the intellectual development of your baby. As he discovers new abilities, activities, and skills, give him the opportunity to practice them, because experience is what shapes the brain. This does not mean you can create a star football player by endless practice and encouragement. For repetition to be effective, it must emphasize whatever interests him. Your challenge is to recognize his interests and provide suitable opportunities for him to master new skills. Learning is best accomplished in an atmosphere of fun and play, not in regimented, highly structured drills. Teach your baby by example: show him that you are sincerely interested in his activity. Let his reward be his new-found information and rejoice with him in that.

PART I: AGELESS ACTIVITIES

Chapter 1 — Is There Intelligent Life Down There?

What is intelligence? A newborn opens her mouth and turns her head when her cheek is touched. Is that intelligence? A baby smiles in recognition of her father as he enters the room. Is that intelligence? An eight-month-old pulls herself up by the sofa's edge to reach a toy on the cushions. Is that intelligence? A toddler pretends to sip tea from an imaginary cup. Is that intelligence? Do they actually *think*? If so, when do they start, and what do they think about?

One dictionary defines intelligence as "the ability to learn or understand or to deal with new or trying situations."[6] Using this definition, it can be said that babies are the very picture of intelligence itself. Babies have a tremendous ability to learn and deal with the new and trying situation of the world outside the womb. Yet the way in which they understand may be quite different from that of most adults.

DIFFERENT KINDS OF INTELLIGENT[7]

Some researchers believe that people, including babies, can have different kinds of intelligence. One baby may have social intelligence, being very sensitive to how others around her feel. Another baby may have musical intelligence; another may have numerical or mathematical intelligence. Others may have spatial intelligence, being very good at perceiving how an object relates to the things around it. While it can be beneficial to notice your baby's strong points, it is more important to encourage her to be involved with a variety of interesting toys and activities. Give her opportunities to enjoy all kinds of satisfying play, experimenting, and exploration. Let her take the lead in playing, and you can relish the beauty of discovering the world all over again through the eyes of your own beautiful child.

Are newborns,. babies, or toddlers thinking? If thinking involves conceiving ideas, forming plans or opinions, and visualizing concepts, it may be more accurate to say that newborns are intelligent creatures who are *learning* to think. However, with the appropriate stimuli at the appropriate stage of intellectual development, they most certainly can think by the time they are toddlers.

It may be difficult for adults to understand existence without thought. Before babies can actually form intentions and images in their brains, they do a remarkable job of processing information from the world around them. They learn! Although children will continue to gain knowledge, hopefully throughout their entire lives, the neural pathways that provide the ability to store and use that knowledge are formed during infancy, the toddler, and preschool years. The processes of beginning to think and learn are nearly completed by the time your child enters first grade.

Babies begin to learn even before they are born. The fetal brain begins registering information long before birth. Your unborn child hears, tastes, senses light, reacts to touch, learns, and remembers. Infants as young as one hour old can demonstrate preferences to stories and music heard in the womb. They are calmed by the familiar voices of their parents, especially if the parents spoke or read to them during the last three months of pregnancy. Once babies are born, their brains not only grow in physical dimension, but they develop faster intellectually than at any other time in their lives.

PLAY IT AGAIN, PLEASE

Psychologist Dr. Anthony DeCasper of the University of North Carolina performed one experiment using a nipple that registered the rate and pressure of an infant's sucking. The infants learned to choose recorded sounds they wanted to hear by changing the way they sucked on the nipple. A newborn only an hour or two old chose the voice of his father, the voice of his mother, and the sound of his mother's heartbeat! Those recordings calmed and reassured the newborn.

In a similar experiment, children's mothers read aloud the story *The Cat in the Hat* twice a day during the last six and a half weeks of their pregnancies. The babies were given the special nipple shortly after birth which allowed them to choose between *The Cat in the Hat* and another story they had never heard, *The King, the Mice, and the Cheese*. In every case the babies selected the familiar story as their story of choice.[8]

At birth, your baby's brain is one quarter the size of your brain, but it triples in size during her first year. However, the size and weight of her brain does not determine her intelligence. The number of connections in her brain does. During the first few months of life, your baby's neural connections multiply exponentially. Her brain creates far more connections than she will ever use in her lifetime in a process described as blooming. During adolescence the connections that have not been reinforced by use and repeated experience are eliminated; this process is known as pruning.[9]

Some have described these processes as an example of survival of the fittest in use-it-or-lose-it philosophy. Others view it as a sculptor starting with a large mass of clay and stripping away the excess to reveal a beautiful new creation. The important thing is: These connections are being formed in the early years. "A one-year-old's brain develops much more rapidly than that of a three-year-old, and a three-year-old's brain develops more rapidly than a six-year-old's."[10] Therefore, the earlier the baby is started in an enriched environment, the more she will benefit from it, and the more opportunity she will have to reinforce or "hard wire" her brain power permanently. Conversely, once certain developmental windows of opportunity close, your baby has missed out forever and will never be all that she could have been.[11]

HOW BABIES LEARN

Babies, like adults, learn through experience. However, babies experience things differently than adults do. They learn about things by how they taste, smell, feel, sound, and so on. What may seem to you to be random limb flailing or banging of toys is actually a learning experience. It takes time to learn to operate the human body, and only an intelligent human can do so. That is, in fact, what your baby is doing when she wildly waves her limbs with or without toys. She is learning how the object (including her own hands, arms, legs, etc.) feels and reacts in situations.

WHERE ARE THE INSTRUCTIONS FOR THIS THING?

Author Sidney Ledson gave an excellent illustration in his book *Raising Brighter Children*.[12] Imagine trying to operate a complex machine, like your family car, without ever having ridden in one, driven one, or even seen it in use. The human body is far more complex than a car, and your newborn baby has to learn to operate it without any experience or instruction. Can you explain to him how to make his arm move?

So, just because he does not have it all figured out yet, that does not mean he is not very bright. On the contrary, it takes quite a brain to teach itself to accomplish such a monumental task.

As mentioned earlier, your baby receives intellectual stimulation from each of her senses, and each form of sense stimulation is important. For example, the importance of visual stimulation was demonstrated in studies done with kittens. The kittens' eyes were sealed during the early months of life. When their eyes were opened, the kittens remained blind because their brains had not received the necessary visual input to hard wire sight as a permanent function of the brain.[13] Unfortunately, similar results have been documented in babies born with cataracts clouding their vision. If the cataracts are not corrected promptly, the babies never develop the power of sight.*

After reading information like that, some parents may go to the other extreme, assaulting their children with constant visual stimulation, hoping to prevent blindness. Many parents tend to react similarly with other forms of intellectual stimulation. The April 28, 1997 issue of *Newsweek* reported on the research of Zero to Three (a child advocacy group) with the following: "87 percent [of parents] think that the more stimulation a baby receives, the better off he will be. In fact, talking, reading, singing, and playing must be carefully matched to a child's level of development, temperament and mood, or the child will tune out or even cringe from the interaction."[14]

Activity suggestions are provided in the second half of this manual for educational play, but you should never try to force them on your child. Suppose your toddler is placing a variety of things on top of the dome lid of her toy box: balls, blocks, stuffed animals. She's fascinated by the varying speeds at which each item falls or rolls off. Bored, you may prefer to teach her to sort socks by color. By following her lead and postponing the sorting lesson, you encourage a very important learning process, and you reinforce that you value her interests.

TUNING IN TO YOUR BABY

How do you allow your baby to initiate activities, and how can you recognize her interests? That depends on her age. As an infant, you primarily will need to present objects for her inspection. If she looks away, closes her eyes, cries, or shows other signs of irritation, then you should put the object away. She may need a break or she may prefer some other item. As your baby becomes more mobile, you can simply have objects and activities available for her to pursue.

How then can parents encourage the right type of learning at the right time? A few general principles apply. First, newborns, babies,

* Eye exams can be given to babies as young as two weeks old. Exams detect vision problems which could lead to an eye(s) not forming functional connections with the brain. Regular medical care is important to all aspects of your baby's health and development.

and toddlers must be allowed to initiate their own actions and choose their own interests. Parents are always obligated to guide and protect their children. Nevertheless, too much "guidance" can result in children losing their joy of learning. Trying to force achievement from a child before she can produce the expected results can frustrate parent and child. Secondly, variety is not only the spice of life, it is the vital nutrient of growing minds. The greater the variety (not necessarily the quantity) of stimulants, the more experience the child gains, the more she learns.

Babies also learn an enormous amount from social interaction. Their attitudes, behaviors, and general emotional makeups are molded by their social environments. Loving human contact, emotional support, encouragement, frequent genuine smiles, kind facial expressions, and warm tones of voice are crucial to every aspect of a baby's development. Brighter children often comprehend weighty subjects before they have the emotional maturity to cope with such knowledge. Therefore, parents must be extremely sensitive to the emotional needs of their child and be willing to explain basic principles for surviving in a harsh environment outside the home. Since this aspect of parenting involves both religious teachings and personal philosophies on life, this program leaves the instilling of this and other moral values as a responsibility of parents and does not address it here. Parents are, however, strongly encouraged not to overlook this vital role.

TEMPERAMENT

Your child's arrival brings with it many exciting and even nerve-wracking experiences. At first you may feel that life as you knew it has come to an end since everything now revolves around the special needs of your baby. Eventually, though, with loving guidance from you, your baby will soon be happy to accept that she is a new member of an already existing household. You can make that household a healthy place for her to grow . . . physically, emotionally, intellectually, spiritually, and socially. This program describes the proper steps for promoting her intellectual growth, but many of the suggestions found herein overlap with her physical, emotional, and social growth as well.

Studies show that there are many factors that influence your baby's temperament. Without a doubt, genetics do play a role in the type of baby you have. Yet other factors are also at work. Dr. Candace Erickson, Director of Behavioral and Developmental Pediatrics at Columbia

The book *Your Baby's Mind*[16] also provided the following important guidelines for baby care:

1. Remember that every child is different. Never mentally or verbally compare children to one another. Each child is wonderful as an individual.

2. Present toys and activities to your baby that are physically safe for his age and that are appropriate for his current stage of development.

3. Try to avoid distractions and interruptions. Answering machines are a modern marvel and childhood does not last forever.

4. Avoid negative, non-constructive criticism. When your child looks to you for advice or seems frustrated, offer positive comments and helpful suggestions.

5. Maintain plenty of eye contact with your baby with smiles in abundance.

6. Rejoice with your baby in his success. He does a great job of scattering blocks. What a thrill when he learns to stack one on top of another.

7. Give clear directions in words your baby can easily understand. Using short, simple sentences with the appropriate tone will help him learn the language, as well as what he should do.

8. Think safety first. Then, be flexible in accepting unexpected uses of toys and household objects. That burp cloth makes a stunning hat!

9. When your baby looks puzzled or confused, that means he is learning. He recognizes that something does not fit into the categories of things he already knows.

10. Your baby learns much through repetition. Encourage him to continue to drop the toy you have already handed him fourteen times.

11. If your baby loses interest in or becomes frustrated with an activity, help him start from that point at another time. For instance, he rolled a truck with one block on top, then two, then three. Since he could not keep three on as long as he liked, help him start with three blocks next time.

12. If necessary, guide your baby to a similar yet simpler activity. It would be simpler to put shapes into the big opening of a shape sorter rather than the individually shaped openings. That way he can become accustomed to putting something in something else before he can actually determine which shapes fit each opening.

13. Demonstrate educational play. Show him how to stack the blocks, and let him unstack them to see how they went together.

14. Present your baby with the next challenge before he becomes bored with his current challenge. This will require you to recognize his signals. Just as you learn which cry means he is hungry and which cry means he is sleepy, you will learn when your child is losing interest in an activity ... if you stay involved.

15. Encourage your baby to make new groupings and links between activities and toys. Blocks can make up one group, and rings can make up another; or, blue blocks and rings can make up one group and red blocks and rings can make another.

16. Exult with your baby when he shares and plays well with others.

17. Without doing the playing for your baby, make yourself available to thrill to his thrills and offer support for his problems.

18. Be attentive to your baby's every form of expression, whether verbal or in body language.

INDEPENDENT, SORT OF

Sometimes when you try to play with your baby, he may get frustrated. If you leave the room, he follows you. The solution: he plays near you while you each do your own thing. He learns to entertain himself; you get some work done. If he has trouble, you are right there to help. If things are going well, you are there to congratulate him.

19. If your baby does not do things as you expected, avoid displaying disappointment or impatience. Offer "positive reinforcement and unconditional affection." Your 10-month-old can empty his toy box, but he will not fill it. Realize that his changing his environment gives him a sense of control in a very big world. Squeal with delight at his beautifully re-decorated floor. Give him a big hug, then show him how much fun it can be to toss the toys back into the box.

20. Focus on activities that seem to most interest your baby. You really wanted to show him how a stack of bowls fit inside one another. He is fascinated with a ball he bumped. Show him the exciting things a ball can do. We all learn more about subjects we care about.

University, lists family development as one such factor.[15] Every member of the family is at a different stage of human development when a baby brings her own unique personality and abilities to the household. This factor explains one of the reasons why children raised in the same household can be so dramatically different.

Although you may not be able to change your baby's temperament, how you view her temperament can greatly affect the happiness of your home *and* your baby's intellectual development. Adopt the attitude that there is no good or bad temperament; there is your temperament, your baby's temperament, and the temperaments of other members of the household. Rather than viewing a placid baby as lazy or non-energetic, appreciate her ability to be completely at ease in her surroundings and her admirable trait of placing relatively few demands on you. Likewise, if your baby is easily startled, is more needy than most babies her age, and is frequently tearful, appreciate her alertness and the opportunity she provides you to fill her world. Whether your baby's temperament matches yours or not, it is up to you as the adult caregiver and loving parent to adapt, while still providing guidance. As long as you allow your own instinctive love and compassion to be the motivating force in your child-rearing decisions, you will foster the growth of a happy, successful individual.

CHAPTER SUMMARY

Do you remember the importance of the following points in your baby's intellectual development?

- Her care and environment.
- Time-appropriate enrichment.
- Intellectual stimulation from each of your baby's senses.
- Allowing her to initiate her own actions and choose her own interests.
- Variety in intellectual stimulation.
- Social interaction.
- Sensitivity to her emotional needs.
- Making the household a healthy place for her to grow.
- How you view her temperament.
- Being flexible while still providing guidance.

Chapter 2 — That Special Bond

If you have ever read anything about caring for a newborn, you have no doubt seen the bonding process described in great detail, along with the importance of physical contact. The knowledge scientists have gained in this aspect of child development has affected the entire birthing practices in most of the advanced cultures of the world. More and more hospitals now make it their policy to encourage as much physical contact between parents and newborns as possible, as soon as possible. Such contact has been found to reduce infant crying, increase infant growth, increase affection, and increase self-confidence on the part of the parents. Usually, cesarean births are implemented only when medically necessary and are performed without general anesthesia. Doing so allows mothers to be as alert as possible and available for spending those precious first moments with their newborns.

Without undermining the importance of early bonding, experts do agree that there is no reason for mothers who must have general anesthesia, cesarean births, or who have premature babies to feel guilty or upset about the lost bonding time. The bonding process is lifelong. Missing the first few hours or even the first few months should not mean that parents give up on bonding with their babies.

WHAT AND HOW IMPORTANT IS IT?

Bonding has been described as the beginning of a love affair between parents and their child. Many parents experience love at first sight of their tiny new miracle. Many others begin the bonding process before the child is even born. They read to their unborn child, talk to him, play music for him, sing to him, and play with him by rubbing protruding feet, hands, and heads as they bulge noticeably around the mother's abdomen. Other parents, because of various factors in their own lives, may need to work at developing this special relationship with their newborns. Regardless of which parent you are, be sure of this: bonding with your child as early and as strongly as you can is an absolute necessity to his positive development. There are no shortcuts. He needs your quality time and plenty of it. Find a way to form this emotional link.

Bonding has been found to directly affect emotional and physical development in children. It even affects their adult futures. *Men's Health*, June 1992, says: "Hugs and physical affection with parents strongly predict successful friendships, marriages and careers in a child's future, says a 36-year study published in the *Journal of Personality and Social Psychology*. Seventy percent of the kids with affectionate parents did well for themselves socially, compared with only 30 percent of the kids with cold-fish parents; and Dad's hugs were found to be as important as Mom's."[17] Through receiving love, your baby learns to love.

Research shows that mothers who had more contact with their babies during the first three days were significantly more affectionate with their babies through the first year. Fathers who are actively involved in their babies' care during the first three days are, one month later, more sensitive to the babies' behavior and feel more involved. In fact, one year later, the father is significantly more attached to his baby and to the mother and is more involved in his baby's care and education. This also affects the father's self-esteem in a positive way, giving him more confidence in his performance as a father and parent.[18]

WHAT CAN YOU DO?

For mothers, breast-feeding is an important way to bond with her baby. As a mother gazes lovingly into her baby's eyes, talks lovingly to him, cuddles him, and pets his skin, she fosters her own maternal instincts while promoting a strong bond of love and intimacy with her baby. Breast-fed babies also feel safe and loved. Fathers are not left out! Dr. T. Berry Brazelton says, "Every child needs . . . a father, and every father can make a difference."[19] Dr. Brazelton also states that where there is an active, involved father, the child's IQ is higher by the time he reaches six or seven years old.

Infants have a strong need to communicate. Until your baby can verbally express himself using words you understand, he must find other ways to communicate. You can begin to open the lines of communication and share fully in the bonding process by showering your baby with hugs and kisses. Laughing, talking, singing, rocking, reading to him, and holding his hand all contribute to bonding. Try to make eye contact with him when you express affection.

Bonding requires genuine, loving concern and interest on your part. Mechanically tending to your baby's physical needs neglects his emotional needs. Changing diapers, feeding, bathing, and putting him to sleep all provide excellent opportunities to form an emotional tie with him. Let him feel real care. Make emotional contact.

HOW DOES IT WORK?

When *responding* to emotions, your baby's brain seems to use the same neural circuits that it uses to *generate* emotion. Therefore, when you return his positive emotional reactions, you reinforce them. For example, he squeals with delight when you pick him up to play; you respond with excited laughter, indicating that you are as excited about this opportunity as he is. Or, he stares in amazement at a sight he has never seen before; you respond with a sincere "ooooh" and "wow," asking "What is it?" Maybe, he smiles at you and you smile back with a hug. Such a pattern of reinforcement beneficially alters the way he will think and conduct himself for the rest of his life.

Just as your positive reactions benefit your baby, tense or negative reactions harm him. Parents who respond to baby's cries with compassionate, soothing sounds and actions form closer bonds than do parents who react in a distressed or hurried manner. This principle applies to any caregiver.

BONDING WITH OTHER CAREGIVERS

Zero to Three recommends that child care be given with at least one caregiver for every three infants and one caregiver for every four toddlers between the ages of 18 and 24 months.[20] You do not want your child in the care of someone who is so overwhelmed with the responsibilities of caring for so many needy little lives that they merely react with irritation to your baby's cry for attention. You want someone who promptly and attentively cares for his needs.

Experts have found that not only *can* babies bond with non-parental caregivers, but they *should* bond with those who care for them on a regular basis. Choose a caregiver that will be there consistently for your baby. Although some people mistakenly believe that exposure to many caregivers will broaden a child's social circle, studies show that babies must be able to bond with caregivers in order to thrive; and bonding takes time. Request that only one or two people be assigned to your baby's care and that those people be caregivers who will be around for the length of time you intend to have him enrolled at that particular establishment.

Thus, if child care outside the home is necessary, be alert to the manner in which the caregiver reacts to your baby. The caregiver's approach will effect your baby's development.

One study by Soviet researcher M. I. Lisina found that babies who were spoken to affectionately, smiled at, and caressed reached "a significantly higher developmental level" than babies who were not treated this way. Dr. Lisina states, "We believe interaction with other people is critically important in the genesis of [a baby's] verbal functions."[21] On the other hand, babies with depressed mothers (during the baby's first year of life), have lower cognitive abilities at four years of age.[22]

Babies of most depressed mothers are said to develop "sad brains." The portion of your baby's brain which controls emotion has little activity in the region related to joy and happiness if he does not witness and experience joy and happiness.[23] Yet not all babies of depressed mothers become indifferent or sad. Mothers who get help for their depression or who rise above their depression when they care for their babies enjoy happy babies.* (For important information about preventing, identifying, and treating postpartum depression, please see Appendix C.) Another way to counteract the effects of a mother's depression is to involve other compassionate caregivers, especially the baby's father. A loving, attentive father can be a tremendous help to both mother and baby.

Logic dictates that, because positive thinking and emotions can be reinforced, so can negative thinking, emotions, and behavior. Stressful, threatening, and frightening experiences are processed in a part of your baby's brain that puts him on alert and awakens his fight-or-flight instincts. If certain tones of voice or household sounds have signaled a bad experience before, your baby will begin to react in a defensive manner before the experience ever reaches the rational part of his brain. This too has been shown to retard intellectual development. Furthermore, children under stress experience increased levels of a steroid called cortisol, which can actually destroy brain cells and have a negative impact on neural connections in certain parts of the brain.[24]

---

* Depression varies in severity with every person, and no one can just "snap out" of clinical depression. If you suffer from depression at any level, seek medical attention. In addition to doing so, some mothers are able to put on a smile and use warm, loving, happy tones when dealing with their babies, despite their depression.

CHAPTER SUMMARY

Do you remember the importance of the following points regarding bonding and your baby's intellectual development?

- Physical contact.
- Early, strong bonding experiences.
- Parental involvement during the first three days of your baby's life.
- Breast-feeding.
- Communication.
- Eye contact.
- Genuine loving concern and interest.
- Making emotional contact while caring for his physical needs.
- Reinforcing his positive emotional reactions.
- Responding to his distress with compassion.
- Bonding with multiple caregivers.

Chapter 3 — Close Encounters

Although mothers and fathers generally differ in the way they handle their babies, both types of attention are vital to healthy babies. Mothers tend to be more nurturing and protective, whereas fathers tend to be more playful. Both roles aid in the baby's development emotionally and intellectually. Researchers have found that children who had fathers who were actively involved with them in a positive way were "consistently rated ahead of schedule developmentally, in problem-solving skills and in social skills ... [C]hildren who were raised by actively involved fathers scored higher in verbal abilities than children raised in homes where fathers were mostly preoccupied with breadwinning."[25] The late Norma Radin, Ph.D. believed that "there's a strong connection between kids' math skills and the amount of contact they have with their fathers."[26] The improved math skills are speculated to be a possible result of roughhousing and sport-like activity that leads to a firmer grasp of spatial relationships. The better interpersonal skills are thought to be a result of learning self-discipline (what rough play is acceptable and what is not) and self-confidence (fathers tend to allow more freedom of movement and activity than do mothers).

One study from an unusual source demonstrated the importance of physical contact. Anthropologists studying Pacific island cultures found this: "When anthropologists study such nonaggressive societies, we observe that it is principally through their child-rearing practices that they produce cooperative, non-violent personalities. Great affection is lavished on children. From infancy on, small children are scarcely ever out of bodily contact with someone who is either cuddling or carrying them."[27] The December 1979 issue of *Psychology Today* stated that "during formative periods of brain growth, certain kinds of sensory deprivation — such as a lack of touching and rocking by the mother — result in incomplete or damaged development of the neuronal systems that control affection."[28] So do not hold back. Love your baby all you can.

Studies have yet to demonstrate a direct link between physical contact and the human immune system. However, it has been shown that physical contact is at least one component of interaction that does have a very real effect on physiological changes, including the immune system. Researchers do admit that, because it appears to have such a close relationship with social attachment and bonding, touch probably affects the immune system through the autonomic nervous system rather than forming a direct link.[29]

JUST TO BE CLOSE TO YOU

An April 21, 1997 segment of ABC's *Good Morning America* chronicled the life of a child named Julianna adopted from a Romanian orphanage at the age of three. The orphanage routinely bound children in their cribs and the babies received only a few minutes of human contact each day. The child's adoptive mother stated that she expected their new daughter to experience developmental delays, but felt that with love and medical attention Julianna would catch up in about six months. At the time of the broadcast, Julianna was eight years old and still "unable to speak in sentences, make friends, or do the simplest things." Doctors expressed their belief that there is still hope for Julianna because "the brain keeps connecting itself into old age" and because Julianna's mother has not given up hope. Dr. Michael Gullen cited the example of children around the same age as Julianna who have had half of their brains removed due to epilepsy. Those children's remaining brain compensated for the missing half. Nevertheless, the importance of physical contact and bonding during the first three years of life is dramatically demonstrated in Julianna's case.[30]

PLAY

For at least fifteen minutes every day, play with your baby. Make this play time involve just you and her, with lots of eye contact and without toys. There is no age limit on this activity. If you can get her to give you fifteen minutes of complete attention every day when she is fifteen, congratulations!

MASSAGE

Massage your baby for about fifteen minutes every day, especially when she wakes up from a nap, to stimulate her developing muscles. For more information, see the section on massage in the next chapter. Additionally, books and classes on infant massage are widely available through hospitals, bookstores, libraries, and the internet.

BABY WEARING

Baby wearing is the term coined to describe carrying your baby in a body sling or pouch-like carrier. Although this parenting practice is fairly foreign to North America, it is quite common in many other parts of the world. Before dismissing this practice as strange or backward, you owe it to yourself and your baby to consider what the experts have to say about it.

Recent studies have shown that, compared to using plastic carseat-type carriers, baby wearing produces a number of significant advantages to parents and babies.[31] These advantages include:

1. Babies and parents enjoy closer emotional attachment;

2. Baby wearers tend to be more attentive to their babies;

3. Babies carried in car-seat type carriers tend to be more vocal in attempting to get their parents' attention (which means worn babies cry less); and

4. Babies worn on the caregiver's body have a constantly moving view of the world around them. This factor has been found to dramatically increase brain maturity over babies who spend much of their time in cribs or playpens. This does not mean that you should never place your baby in cribs or playpens. To the contrary, babies need time alone in these areas to exercise their limbs and to learn to entertain themselves. Carseat-type carriers also serve a useful purpose and should not be excluded entirely. However, what is being emphasized here is the benefit of regular baby wearing.

Specific Benefits to Your Baby

Have you ever wondered why rocking your newborn has such a calming effect? Have you wondered why toys and audio cassettes that play recordings of a human heartbeat have become so popular among new parents? The answer to both of these questions is this: Babies are reminded of the security they felt in the womb. Baby wearing combines these benefits with physical contact to make your baby feel right at home.

Wearing her has another health benefit for your baby, according to Susan Ludington-Hoe, Ph.D., of the University of Maryland at Baltimore School of Nursing.[32] Newborns, preemies, and distressed or crying babies have fast, irregular heartbeats. When you wear your baby, she can achieve a state of "entrainment," which means that, as she listens to your breathing and heartbeat, her own heartbeat slows down and synchronizes with yours. In addition, your familiar scent, gait, and sounds can help her fall into a "quiet sleep state," during which her brain matures. Because babies' brains experience so much physical growth during the first year, they need as much of this regenerative down time as possible.

Ordinarily, most babies spend an increasing amount of time crying each day until they reach a peak at six weeks of age. After that, they spend decreasing amounts of time crying each day. This is the case in Western societies, such as the United States, where newborns and babies are carried an average of nearly three hours per day. *Studies have shown that, when babies are carried merely one-and-a-half additional hours per day, crying decreased by up to 43%; and rather than a peak of crying at six weeks of age, there was a steady decline in crying right from the very beginning.* Interestingly, the babies did not cry less frequently; instead the babies merely cried for shorter periods of time. Length of crying sessions is often one of the greatest causes of stress in new parents. Therefore, shortening these sessions by carrying your child more, regardless of whether she is asleep or awake, crying or content, can greatly improve the overall parenting experience and make a happier baby.[33]

Concerns

Well-meaning friends and family members may try to convince you that wearing your baby will spoil her and that she should be left in a carrier, crib, or playpen. As mentioned above, research shows quite the opposite: sling-worn babies cry 43% less than babies left on their own. Experts testify that baby wearing often results in babies having a greater sense of security, improved social skills, and increased cognitive development.[34] Why? Largely because of their increased exposure to the world and the people in it, as well as the additional involvement and attentiveness of their parents. Recent findings explode another myth, as well: Contrary to what your in-laws may tell you, rather than delaying your baby's ability to crawl and walk, baby wearing actually enhances motor development.[35] So your baby seems to benefit all the way around; but what about you?

Specific Benefits to You

If you are her mother, wearing your baby makes you more attentive to her. This is not just a matter of her being literally six inches in front of you. Her continued presence causes you to produce high levels of "mothering" hormones, such as prolactin and oxytocin. That means your baby receives better quality care. In fact, studies have shown that "mothers who wear their babies are less prone to postpartum depression." Also, if your baby tends to be colicky or just needy in general, you will be better able to handle the stress of her crying because you will be more aware of what calms and comforts her.

Working parents receive important benefits from baby wearing. After being away from their babies for hours at a time, most parents come home to a load of additional duties that require attention. Wearing your baby will allow you to include her in your activities. You can talk to her as you go through your routine and share valuable time with her that may otherwise be missed. Also, requiring your baby's caregiver to wear her for a given period of time each day ensures that she receives precious physical contact throughout her time away from you.

For Everybody?

Baby wearing may not be for every parent or for every child. Some babies hate being worn and are still happy children. Some babies prefer to continue as a parent's appendage. However, noted child expert Dr. William Sears advises parents to give baby wearing a genuine effort before resigning themselves to the idea that it is not for their child.[36] If your baby seems resistant to the sling or pouch-like carrier at first, try using it for just a few minutes at a time for a while, gradually building up the amount of time your baby can be worn. Dr. Sears believes that most babies will come around, but he also cautions that "if it's not working, drop it." Just because it is a beneficial aid to many does not mean that it is a requirement.

The type of sling or pouch-like carrier you choose may also affect your experience. Try a number of different kinds to ensure a comfortable fit. Be conscious of the fabric, also. A heavy fabric that makes you hot and uncomfortable is likely to affect your mood and possibly add strain to your muscles. Dr. Sears recommends that parents with back problems use a sling in the cradle hold (similar to a nursing position) or the snuggle hold (chest-to-chest) positions.

BABY WEARING SAFETY

DOs

When you first begin baby wearing or when your baby is still a newborn, be sure to continue to support her with at least one arm/hand. Later you will acquire the ability to have both hands free during baby wearing.

Make sure the sling or pouch-like carrier covers your baby's back at least to the top of her shoulder blades so that she does not flip out of it if she suddenly arches her back.

Remember where your baby is as you navigate through doorways and around corners to be sure her head and body are safe.

DON'Ts

Never wear your baby near the stove or while cooking, cycling, or riding in a car. No matter how secure she feels in her sling or carrier, there is no substitute for a good car/bike seat.

Never reach, stretch, or turn without supporting your baby with one arm; you do not want to spill her out of her sling/carrier. Do not bend at the waist for the same reason and for the sake of your back; bend with your knees.

Never drink hot beverages while wearing your baby.

CHAPTER SUMMARY

Do you remember these important points with regard to physical contact and your baby's intellectual development?

- The benefits of the difference in how mothers and fathers interact with their children,
- The result in societies where babies are scarcely out of bodily contact with caregivers,
- The benefits of loving your baby all you can,
- The benefits of physical contact on your baby's immune system,
- The benefits of one-to-one play,
- The benefits of infant massage, and
- The advantages of baby wearing over carseat-type carriers
    - familiar security
    - physical contact
    - entrainment
    - quiet sleep state
    - decreased crying
    - happier baby
    - improved social skills
    - increased cognitive development
    - enhanced motor development
    - more attentive caregivers
    - increased production of "mothering" hormones
    - decreased incidence of postpartum depression
    - greater parental ability to handle the stress of baby crying
    - improved parent-child understanding and
    - increased quality time.

Chapter 4 — The Magic Touch of Massage

Massage affects intellectual growth through two indirect paths: bonding and motor skill development. Though the paths are indirect, the benefits are very real and quite substantial.

BONDING

Massage contributes to intellectual development by enhancing and strengthening the bonding process, which is vital in the early years. No matter how many babies you have cared for or raised before, you have never had *this* baby before. Massage helps you understand your new baby's body language and personality, which improves your ability to respond when something is wrong. As you lovingly rub his tiny hard-working muscles, you will start to see how he reacts when something is pleasant and how he reacts when something is uncomfortable. You will pick up on his preferences: he may find gentle, feathery touches irritating; he may be ticklish; he may consider vigorous massage fun and exciting; he may feel that circular strokes are relaxing. You will know what to use and what to avoid when he is fussy. What a wealth of information you will have at your disposal, and what a loving way to obtain it!

Massage also affords fathers an important opportunity for the physical contact and quality time similar to that of nursing mothers with their babies. Massage is likewise a wonderful bonding opportunity for adoptive parents, foster parents, parents of premature babies, and other parents who, for one reason or another, may have missed out on the early bonding experiences available in uncomplicated deliveries.*

MOTOR SKILL DEVELOPMENT

Second, because infants and babies take in information through their bodies, motor skill development plays a tremendous role in

* Parents of blind children obviously cannot make eye contact with their babies; parents who have never been nurtured themselves may not know how to express loving touch; etc. Massage is a terrific way to bridge that gap.

intellectual development. Cross-cultural studies have found that cultures who massage their infants result in more rapid infant motor development than those who do not provide this muscle stimulation.[37]

I'M NOT A RAT, BUT I COULD STILL USE A GOOD MASSAGE

Researchers found that interrupting mother-baby rat interaction directly affected cell growth, growth hormones, and two other biochemical processes. Is the same true of humans? Premature babies and babies who failed to thrive for nonorganic reasons gained weight and developed better after receiving massage than those without the extra attention.

This study found that the type of mother-baby rat interaction proved vital. Rather than nutritional, visual, auditory, or olfactory, the vital interaction was found to be touch — not the baby's ability to touch the mother, but the mother's active stroking of the baby. Again, researchers found parallel results in human babies. When no physio-biological causes were found for the baby's failure to thrive, the baby returned to normal growth with the affectionate nurturing of pediatric personnel.

A subsequent experiment was performed on premature human babies separated from their mothers to receive special care in a "grower" nursery. The babies who were massaged for three 15-minute periods during three consecutive hours each day for 10 days averaged 47% more weight gain than babies in the nursery who were not massaged. The massaged babies were awake for longer periods of time, more developmentally mature, and required an average of six days less hospitalization than non-massaged babies![38]

Once again, researchers looked to the rats for more information, with startling results: rats that were "handled" experienced biochemical changes that allowed them to manage stress significantly better than rats who were not handled . . . so much so, in fact, that the aging process (particularly loss of memory and brain function) was actually diminished by nearly half the rats' life spans! Further study is now being conducted to determine if there are similar results in humans.[39]

OTHER BENEFITS

Your baby also learns that an adult's touch is not always the painful touch of necessary medical care, such as needle sticks and prodding, but that it can be loving touch designed to stimulate or relax muscles. Your baby receives a number of other benefits as well: stimulated respiratory, circulatory, and digestive systems; gas and colic relief; improved healing due to relief of congestion and pain; improved sleep; stress management and relief; and a feeling of being loved and well-cared for.

TECHNIQUES

There are a variety of massage techniques (*e.g.*, Swedish, Indian, reflexology), as well as a number of massage programs. Massage can even have different purposes, such as either to stimulate or to relax the muscles. Massage involves other factors, as well, like attitude, participation, and preparation. Massage should not be viewed as a matter of routine care, but as a unique opportunity for you and your baby to share special time together. Be alert to his reactions and respect his comfort zone. If he seems annoyed or irritated, try a different approach, talking about it as you continue. Relax yourself before you begin and set aside uninterrupted time so that you can focus on him.

Many massage programs begin by your asking the baby if he wants or is ready for a massage. Even if he is too young to comprehend the question, asking will remind you to be aware of how he feels about the massage. If he initially avoids eye contact, crosses his arms, or tries in some other way to resist the massage, work with him at his pace. Try starting with his feet and legs since they are less vulnerable parts of the body. Use a cold-pressed edible oil on your hands, and give your baby time to adjust to the massage before you proceed to his abdomen, chest, arms, hands, face, and back.

The International Association of Infant Massage Instructors conducts classes to train parents in infant massage around the country. The training consists of about fives sessions, and all family members and caregivers are invited to attend. If you would like more information, you can write to them at their national headquarters: The International Association of Infant Massage Instructors, Post Office Box 16103, Portland, OR, 97216-0103.

CHAPTER SUMMARY

Do you remember the following information with regard to massage and your baby's intellectual development?

- The two indirect ways in which massage improves your child's intellectual development;
- The additional benefits to your baby;
- The benefits to you as a parent;
- The different purposes of particular types of massage;
- Massage techniques;
- How to overcome problems; and
- Sources of additional information and instruction.

Chapter 5 — What about Swimming and Exercise?

Swimming and exercise are linked together here because they are in many ways related. Although each facet is addressed individually, you should know that a policy statement issued by AAP in the late 1980s spoke against the use of elaborate exercise equipment and various exercise programs for infants and babies due to the danger of harming soft, developing bones.[40] However, there are things you can safely do to stimulate your baby's muscles and motor development.

SWIMMING

The issue of whether to teach infants to swim is a matter of intense controversy among child care specialists and swimming educators. The benefits of teaching your baby to swim are fairly obvious: she will be in less danger of drowning in case she accidentally falls into water; you and she will have another environment for creative play and quality time together; swimming is great exercise with little or no harmful impact on developing bones and muscles; and swimming is a favorite recreation of many.

However, the dangers of teaching your baby to swim are far too serious to be ignored. One of the most frightening dangers is the threat of hyponatremia, or water intoxication.[41] Water intoxication occurs when infants or babies ingest too much water, fail to excrete enough water, or both. While it is very difficult for adults to take in too much water, it is not difficult at all for babies, since they cannot filter the water as fast as older children and adults. In fact, babies who are fed breast milk only should not have any water at all for at least the first four months, unless directed otherwise by their pediatricians. (See the nutritional information in Chapter 7 — Brain Food.) Babies who are fed formula are at risk of becoming malnourished if given additional water, since it can dilute the necessary nutrition in the formula. Regardless of how your baby is fed, excess water dilutes the sodium in the blood. When this happens, the body can no longer function properly and your baby can suffer an altered mental state, abnormally low body temperature, bloating, and possibly seizures.

Another significant danger of teaching your infant or baby to swim is that it may result in a false sense of security for you as her parents or for others entrusted with her care. No child can be "drown-proofed," and overconfidence in your baby's skills can be disastrous.

Also, many dispute whether children retain the swimming skills they were taught while infants or babies.

In view of the risks involved, it is highly recommended that you not try to teach your baby to swim yourself. If you do decide to have your baby taught to swim, you may do well to visit the website of Harvey Barrett, Ph.D. at www.infantswim.com. His method is recommended by David Carr, MD, because it was developed through experience, research, and refinement. At the time of Baby E.D.'s research and development, Infant Swimming Research, Inc. claimed to have taught over 70,000 infants and toddlers water survival skills without a single significant accident. Babies must be at least six months old and able to crawl. Qualified instructors teach babies and toddlers in the program to propel themselves through the water, roll onto their backs to get air, and grab the side of the pool to breathe.

EXERCISE

Books devoted to various programs for baby exercise and gymnastics are readily available on the market. Most include massage, as discussed in the previous chapter. Use care when selecting an exercise program for your baby, keeping in mind the previously mentioned warning by AAP regarding babies' soft bones. A program of infant and baby massage that strengthens your baby's muscles and reinforces bonding might be best.

Toddlers are naturally full of energy and will challenge you to keep up with *them*. There are definite ways to encourage this activity to be a healthy experience without forming a structured exercise routine. All you need to do is provide the space and the opportunity for your toddler; if she has a tendency to be passive or inactive, encourage her to discover physical activities. Avoid using television as a babysitter. Rather, provide her with toys and activities that promote her development of strength, coordination, and agility: push/pull toys, cars/trucks with sound effects, balls of various sizes, a tricycle, crawling games (in and out of cardboard boxes or playground equipment), and roughhouse activities on a soft surface with you.

CHAPTER SUMMARY

Do you remember the following information with regard to teaching your baby to swim and exercising your baby?

- The benefits of teaching your baby to swim;
- The dangers of teaching your baby to swim;
- Who should teach your baby to swim; and
- Whether exercise programs for babies are necessary or advisable.

Chapter 6 — Spoiled Baby, Oxymoron

Does constant attention to your newborn spoil him? Before that question can be answered, spoiling must first be defined. Webster's dictionary lists among its definitions for spoiling: "impair[ing] disposition or character of by overindulgence or excessive praise; pamper[ing] excessively; coddl[ing] (to treat with extreme care)."[42] By the latter definition, babies must be spoiled because they must be treated with extreme care. But will it damage his disposition or character? Is it possible to overindulge a baby with excessive praise or pampering?

Leading experts agree that if a child is spoiled, it must no longer be a baby; and if it *is* a baby, it *cannot* be spoiled. Spoiling your child during the first four to six months is practically impossible. Some experts claim that it is impossible to spoil him during the entire first year. In fact, they further agree that babies who receive prompt, loving responses to their cries actually cry less and sleep better than children who feel like their pleas for help and attention either go unnoticed or provoke hostile reactions. Babies are not capable of forming intentions such as crying for attention before six months of age. Therefore, your baby's cries before then will always have a physical cause rather than a manipulative one.

Just as mirroring your baby's positive emotional behavior reinforces the pleasing circuits of his brain, so responding to your baby's needs in a soothing way establishes mental pathways that he will use to soothe himself. He will literally learn that his situation is not necessarily as horrible as he may at first feel it is. Thus, you make life easier on yourself and for him in the long run if you respond attentively with genuine concern and compassion when he cries.

Around six months of age your baby will start becoming increasingly independent. If, at that time, you meet his every need before he even becomes aware of it or if you hover over him jumping at his every grunt, you may inadvertently retard his development. Exploration and curiosity should be encouraged. How will your child learn problem-solving skills if he is never allowed to encounter any problems? The activities recommended in the age-related chapters are designed to provide your baby with the appropriate amount of intellectual stimulation. This stimulation will be enough to promote intellectual growth without causing him frustration and an overwhelming sense of failure.

Experts have determined how much babies can handle at approximate ages. However, you must get to know your baby's personality. Learn to recognize his signals. In order to communicate with him during the preverbal months (before he can speak your language), you must learn to understand his facial expressions, body movements, and cries. Babies tend to shut down and go to sleep when over-stimulated. So, if you are familiar with his sleep habits, you will know if it is time for his nap or if he has had all the fun he can stand.

Entire books and videos have been created on the subject of baby signals and are available at your local bookstore, library, and via the internet. If you are not sure whether you are reading your baby's non-verbal signals well enough, or if you would just like confirmation of your own instincts, consult the information available through these sources.

Specific and entire books have been dedicated to the issue of spoiling. Since most of the information on the prevention of spoiling falls within the realm of discipline, this program merely provides recommendations that experts in child care and development generally consider to be constructive.

CHAPTER SUMMARY

Do you remember the importance of the following points with regard to enriching your baby's development and the issue of spoiling?

- Prompt, loving responses;
- Encouraging exploration and curiosity;
- Getting to know your baby's personality;
- Learning to recognize your baby's signals; and
- Consulting additional sources.

Chapter 7 — Brain Food

Throughout human history, trends have been set, reversed, and then reinstated in a seemingly endless cycle. Breast-feeding is one such trend. Although it was the original method of feeding children, breast-feeding was at one time during this century regarded as socially backward. Today, the highest rates of breast-feeding are found among higher-income, college-educated women under the age of thirty.

The more we learn about health and nutrition, the more we must acknowledge that the original method for feeding babies is the best method after all. And, yes, breast-feeding actually stimulates intellectual development! The results of an 18-year study were published in the January 1998 issue of *Pediatrics*.[43] The study found that children who were breast-fed enjoyed higher intelligence quotients (tested at ages eight and nine); increased reading comprehension, mathematical ability, and scholastic ability (tested at ages ten through thirteen); higher ratings by their teachers in reading and mathematics (tested at ages eight and twelve); and higher scores on high school exit exams. Why?

Apparently, this is a result of a combined benefit from better nutrition, maternal bonding, and intellectual stimulation. Recent information suggests that nutritional components found in breast milk that are not found in formula actually play a part in building brain power. Dr. William Sears recommends that breast-feeding women eat tuna or salmon three times a week to increase their intake of certain brain-building compounds.[45]

NURSING AND BRAIN ACTIVITY

Scientists often use pupil activity to measure intellectual and emotional activity in the brain. In doing so, one researcher found that the object causing the greatest pupil dilation in infants less than one month old was the mother's face. Similarly, child psychologist Anne-Marit Duve found that "a high degree of skin stimulation, a high degree of contact — not the least the contact connected with nursing — can stimulate the mental activity, which in turn can lead to greater intellectual capacity in adulthood."[44]

All your baby's senses are at work while she is being nursed: she feels the warmth and smells the scent of her mother's skin; she hears the heartbeat and voice that became so familiar in the womb; her inner ear fluid is set in motion and her sense of balance is stimulated; her eyes take in what has been found to be the most visually stimulating and attractive object for newborn brains — her mother's face at exactly the right distance from hers! She also builds up her powers of concentration and endurance in order to get enough food to survive. There are a number of other benefits of breast-feeding:[46]

1. Breast-feeding meets the exact nutritional needs of your baby: It contains the right proportion of vitamins, minerals, and elements in the composition necessary for her use. It is easily digestible. It contains necessary growth hormones.

2. Breast-feeding helps protect your baby from common diseases, especially viral diseases, throughout the first six months of life. It reduces the incidence and severity of diarrhea, lower respiratory infection, ear infections, bacterial meningitis, botulism, and urinary tract infections. A number of studies show that breast-feeding may also protect against sudden infant death syndrome (SIDS), insulin-dependent diabetes mellitus, Crohn's disease, ulcerative colitis, lymphoma, allergic diseases, and other chronic digestive diseases.

3. Breast-feeding has been found to promote better tooth and jaw development, and the longer the duration of nursing, the greater the chances that the baby's upper and lower teeth will align properly.

4. There are no bottles to sterilize. There are no formulas to buy, to mix, to heat, or to worry about changing as your baby grows. Breast milk is never over diluted or over concentrated by human error in mixing. Breast milk is always sanitary.

5. As long as your baby is with her mother, she need never go hungry.

6. Breast-feeding helps shrink the mother's uterus back to or close to its original size and helps her lose the weight gained during pregnancy.

7. Breast-feeding reduces postpartum bleeding and reduces blood loss over the first few months after delivery by delaying

menstruation. This results in better iron levels for breast-feeding mothers.

8. Women who breast-feed have lower risk of hip fractures after menopause since their bones remineralize better than women who do not breast-feed.

9. Breast-feeding reduces the risk of ovarian and premenopausal breast cancer.

10. Breast-feeding results in healthier babies who need fewer trips to the doctor and in parents who have more time and energy and miss less work for a child's illness.

For additional benefits or more information about the benefits mentioned above, visit ProMoM, Inc.'s website (www.promom.org) for "101 Reasons to Breastfeed Your Child," or write to Promotion of Mother's Milk, Inc., P.O. Box 3912, New York, New York, 10163.

Surprisingly, although breast-feeding is natural, it is not instinctive. New mothers must learn to breast-feed. There are tips and techniques to successful breast-feeding, including baby positioning and breast care. Baby and parenting magazines usually have no short supply of articles offering such information. Many local hospitals and baby stores also provide literature and programs to help overcome difficulties in breast-feeding. The medical field now has an entire branch of lactation specialists. Help is readily available to encourage more mothers to breast-feed their babies. Breast-feeding is truly nursing your baby.

AN UNEXPECTED HAZARD

Recent studies have found a surprising detriment to long-term breast-feeding. Mothers who give their babies pacifiers "tended to breastfeed their babies less frequently" and to experience "inadequate milk supplies."[47] Pacifier use also has possible links to recurrent ear infections and symptoms such as "wheezing, earache, vomiting, fever, diarrhea, and colic."[48]

THE CHOICES

Breast milk is so clearly superior for your baby that even the companies who make baby formulas advocate breast-feeding. But what if you decide to use formula? Does it have to be one or the other, or can there be a compromise? Is it okay to give your baby supplemental food or drinks, like table food, fruit or vegetable juice, water, or cow's milk? Does any of it really make that big of a difference? Absolutely!

Many experts now emphasize that, even if mothers do not intend to breast-feed for any extended period of time, every effort should be made to breast-feed during the first few days. If possible, breast-feeding should begin within one hour of giving birth. The clear or yellowish fluid called colostrum (nicknamed "liquid gold" by some) is produced only during the first two to five days of your baby's life and yields significant benefits to her overall health and development. In fact, mothers of premature babies produce a milk similar to colostrum for much longer than mothers who carried their baby to term because of the special nutritional needs of premature babies. Colostrum gives your baby antibodies and protective cells that fight bacteria and viruses and help protect her from diseases. It also has a special nutrient composition that she can easily digest and that helps her get rid of that tar-like meconium.

THE DANGER OF COW'S MILK

A June 1992 policy statement issued by AAP warns against feeding babies cow's milk during the first year of life. The statement explained that cow's milk lacks the necessary iron, linoleic acid, and vitamin E, and that it contains excessive sodium, potassium, and protein. These nutritional problems are even worse when cow's milk is used in connection with solid foods. Children who do drink cow's milk during the first year of life suffer from significant iron deficiencies, which results in "long-term changes in behavior that may not be reversed even with iron supplementation." AAP's position: "The only acceptable alternative to breast milk is iron-fortified infant formula" during the first year of life.[49]

Breast milk is so perfect for your baby that she will not require any other food or drink for the first six months of life. (See the box on cow's milk above and the footnote on water* below.) In fact, because it is easier for her to drink from a bottle than to nurse, she will breast-feed better if she does not have the opportunity to drink from a bottle during the first six months. AAP even recommends that pacifiers be avoided whenever possible. Further, because breast milk is produced on a supply and demand basis, your baby's nursing less would decrease her supply of breast milk.

* As mentioned in the chapter on swimming, babies cannot process water as well as adults. The latest research indicates that babies should not drink any water during the first four months of life. Between four months and one year of age, they should have no more than four ounces per day (preferably spread throuughout the day) if any.

If your baby is formula-fed, make sure you use an iron-fortified formula. Like breast milk, iron-fortified formula should not be supplemented with water, juice, or table food during the first six months. Water and cow's milk are dangerous, and some recent studies have shown a possible link between earlier feeding of table foods/juice and food allergies later in life.

Because breast milk cannot be measured, you may wonder whether your baby is getting enough to eat. Well-intentioned "helpers" may add to the problem by making comments such as, "Maybe your milk is too weak." "Maybe your milk is too rich." "Maybe you're feeding her too much." "Maybe you're not feeding her enough." As long as your baby is gaining an appropriate amount of weight for her sex and age and the mother is eating and resting properly, your baby is being fed perfectly well. AAP recommends that you keep a record of feedings and diaper changes during the first few days to help her doctor evaluate how you and she are doing.

Your baby should nurse at both breasts each time she is fed, yet she should finish at one breast before being switched to the other. The content of breast milk changes throughout a feeding session. The beginning flow of milk contains a large volume of low-calorie milk. During the feeding, the fat content of the milk increases (your baby needs this fat) and the volume of milk delivered decreases. Therefore, according to the book *Your Child's Development from Birth through Adolescence*, "if a baby is transferred from one breast to the other before she has finished at the first, she may end up taking in too little of the high-calorie milk, and need to be fed more frequently."[50] The total process usually takes 20 to 40 minutes, and some take as long as 60 minutes. The rule of thumb for babies over five days old is: If your baby nurses at least eight times during a 24-hour period and wets at least eight diapers per 24-hour period after feeding, she is getting enough to eat.

WHEN TO WEAN COMPLETELY

WHO, the World Health Organization, recommends breast-feeding your baby as long as possible.[51] AAP also recommends breast-feeding for at least the first year, and as long after that as your family cares to continue.[52]

WHEN BREAST-FEEDING IS NOT BEST-FEEDING

Not every mother should breast-feed her baby. Whatever a mother takes in, the baby takes in. Therefore, if a mother uses drugs or consumes alcohol, the baby would be better off not breast-feeding. It is also vital that nursing mothers continue to eat nutritional meals, get plenty of rest, and consume as little caffeine as possible from conception through the entire breast-feeding period. In addition, mothers who have serious diseases, such as untreated active tuberculosis or AIDS, may be advised by their doctors not to breast-feed. Other than these exceptions, though, experts advise that every mother make the effort to breast-feed her baby.

HOW FATHERS CAN HELP

As a father you may tend to feel a little jealous of the seemingly constant attention your baby receives from her mother. Still, a father who cares about what is best for his baby will reassure and tenderly support his baby's mother by demonstrating his approval of breast-feeding in words and deeds. Breast-feeding is physically demanding and difficulties may arise. Thus, mothers may be tempted to give up. Fathers can support the arrangement physically by helping the mother get sufficient rest and nutrition, helping with household duties, changing/caring for the new baby, and caring for other children in the family. Fathers can help support the arrangement emotionally by keeping the mother as relaxed and happy as possible, since her emotional state has a direct influence on the quality of her milk. This support includes listening to the mother's concerns and offering solutions where necessary.

INTRODUCING SOLIDS

Although many parents find babies' feeding habits unacceptable, meals need not be a battle. When your baby first begins to eat solid food, the mess will probably be confined mostly to her face and bib. Beginning around six to eight months, though, your baby will be fascinated by the disappearance of objects (thus the recommendation of peek-a-boo games). This means that mealtimes present her with wonderfully unique new "toys" of various textures, tastes, smells, and consistencies with which to experiment. Such investigative work is part of the learning process. Rather than trying to stifle her creative activities, take precautions that make them more tolerable. Put a washable mat or liner (even a shower curtain) under her highchair and wait until the end of her meal to clean up the area, rather than repeatedly re-cleaning the area throughout the meal (which, by the way, makes you a target for flying food). Now, the big question: What do you feed her, and when?

Six to Nine Months

Around six months of age,* your baby can gradually begin eating cereals, mashed vegetables, and fruits. Remember, however, that adding supplemental food or drinks to her diet before she reaches the age of six months may contribute to food allergies later in life. When she does start to eat or drink something other than breast milk or formula, you should give her the breast milk or formula first so her nutritional needs are met. Doing so also takes the edge off of her hunger and makes her more receptive to the new experience.

To start, you can mix iron-fortified rice cereal with breast milk or formula for a thin, watery consistency. Your baby can now try pureed fruits and vegetables, as well, such as applesauce, peas, and carrots. Local bookstores and libraries usually carry a good supply of recipe collections and cookbooks for baby food, such as *Feed Me, I'm Yours* by Vicki Lansky[54] and others.

FEEDING THE MIND

When it comes to the effect of infant nutrition on intelligence, there is good news and bad news. The bad news is that even mild undernutrition impairs cognitive function. Infants who suffer from poor nutrition have lower IQ levels, cognitive functions, and school achievement, and the damage is likely to be permanent. The good news is that, if the infants begin receiving adequate nutrition, brain development may actually catch up to some extent on what was missed.[53] Check with a nutritionist or other qualified health care provider to be sure your baby's needs are being met.

If you buy your baby's food, be sure always to spoon the food into a separate bowl or dish rather than serving her directly from the jar. Re-inserting the spoon into the jar after it has been in her mouth contaminates the food that remains in the jar for a later feeding. The

* Your baby is ready when she can: sit up with support, hold her own head steady, and suck in her lower lip when you take a spoon from her mouth. She may still need to learn to swallow food received from the spoon, since a different tongue action is required than for sucking human or artificial nipples.

same goes for bottle-feeding formula or breast milk: always dispose of the remaining contents of a bottle after use.

After a while, you can begin to add barley, wheat, oat, mixed cereals, Cheerios, cooked mushy vegetables, crackers, noodles and pasta, pancakes and waffles, fruits (fresh and canned), and soft bread. Be sure to cut all solids into pieces the size of your pinky fingernail and remove peels and seeds.

Nine to Twelve Months

While still nursing or formula feeding first, you can now give your baby some adult cereal with additional breast milk or formula. Again, remember that babies should not have cow's milk during their first year. She can now have hard-boiled egg yolk, mashed potatoes, ripe fruits and mushy vegetables, soft bread, and soft boneless fish.

Twelve to Twenty-Four Months

If your baby is still nursing, continue to start her meals with breast milk. You can now add the following foods to her diet: cheese, yogurt, cottage cheese, whole cow's milk (no low-fat dairy products before age 2), crackers, toast, whole eggs, cooked hamburger or chicken, fruit, and well-cooked vegetables.

SOMETHING FISHY

Fish is a wonderful part of a healthy diet, but there are safety issues to be considered. Mercury, pesticides, and other toxins contaminate some fish more than others; thus some fish is more dangerous to babies (up to one year old) and pregnant and nursing mothers.

Safety expert for ParentsPlace.com, Sue Gilbert, M.S., offered the following guidelines for enjoying fish safely (based on FDA guidelines):

1. Limit your intake of fresh water fish (particularly inland lakes) as they are more likely to be contaminated . . . Lean ocean fish like cod, flounder and haddock are least likely to be contaminated.

2. Eat smaller, young fish as they have had less time to accumulate toxins in their fat.

3. Eat open ocean, deep water fish or farm raised fish more often than fresh water fish since they are less likely to have been exposed to toxins.

4. Check with the Department of Public Health before eating fish from nearby waters. It may be that local industries have polluted the water and caused unusually high levels of toxins in locally caught fish.

5. If you are a sport fisher, don't eat fish that you catch if you fish the same area over and over.

6. Eat fish from a variety of places.[55]

Choking Hazards

For the first two years, the following foods present choking hazards to your baby: chunks of meat, hot dogs, food with bones, cherries, dried fruit, fruit with pits, raisins, unpeeled fruit, unripe pears, whole grapes, raw or undercooked vegetables, stringy foods, hard beans, nuts, large seeds, peanut butter, pickles, popcorn, potato/tortilla chips, gum, hard candy, and ice cubes.

FOOD ALLERGIES AND LEARNING DISABILITIES

Many people associate food allergies with rashes, diarrhea, vomiting, and/or breathing problems ... with good reason. However, a number of pediatricians and allergists have seen significant improvements in children diagnosed with behavior and learning problems ranging from hyperactivity to autism by eliminating certain foods from the children's diets.[56] If your baby experiences frequent ear or respiratory infections, be sure to consider food allergies as a possible cause. She may have an allergy to or maybe an intolerance for yeast, sugar, dairy, cereal grains, or other foods or food products. Seek appropriate treatment from a physician who recognizes the role of allergy sources and food intolerances in causing bacterial infections. Not all physicians do, for whatever philosophical reasons they may have. Yet, you owe it to your baby and to yourself to examine food allergies as a possible cause of her problems. The important thing is to get *effective* treatment, since chronic ear infections can affect language development.

CHAPTER SUMMARY

Do you remember the following information with regard to how food and nutrition affect your baby's intellectual development?

- How breast-feeding stimulates intellectual development;
- Additional benefits of breast-feeding;
- Help with breast-feeding;
- The importance of colostrum;
- When your baby will need additional food and drink;
- How to know if your baby is getting enough to eat;
- The changing content of breast-milk throughout a feeding;
- When to wean your baby;
- When your baby should not be breast-fed;
- How fathers can help with breast-feeding;
- Tips for making the introduction of solid foods more tolerable;
- Age-specific guidelines for solid foods;
- Choking hazards; and
- The link between food allergies and learning disabilities.

Chapter 8 — Loving Learning Language

Learning a new language is a formidable task for adults, yet it comes naturally to babies. To make the most of that natural (yet temporary) ability, it is vital to talk to your baby throughout the day, every day, from at least as early as birth. Explain what you are doing throughout the day. Describe textures, tastes, feelings, colors. Talking to him will be a delicate balancing act. Babies instinctively tune out stimulation overload. The trick is to supply the right amount of stimulation without making him cringe or shut down. He is the only one who can let you know how much is too much. Watch his reactions. Is he involved in the conversation, or does he seem fussy or sleepy?

In the beginning your baby will not comprehend the meaning of your words. He will, however, learn to speak much more easily. Besides aiding in bonding and creating good parent-child habits, communicating with your baby affords him the ability to learn words before he can speak them and will cause the speech capacity of his brain to greatly increase between six and twelve months of age. This intellectual growth will accelerate even further between twelve and eighteen months when your child begins to actually understand the meaning of words. According to psychiatrist Janellen Huttenlocher of the University of Chicago, the more words a baby hears spoken, the faster he will learn language.[57] But, again, he will not hear the words if he tunes you out; so be balanced.

Your baby is born with certain neural functions "hard wired" or permanently written into his brain, such as the functions that control breathing, heartbeat, and basic motor skills. Language, however, is not automatically programmed. Moreover, learning language is more than just memorizing a large group of words. Language is a complex system for communicating thoughts through sounds, gestures, and the written word. Contrary to what most parents may believe, babies acquire the ability to use language during the first six months, long before they can speak in complete sentences, much less read or write. Yet parents instinctively talk to their infants in exactly the most beneficial way for babies to learn languages. How? In a pattern of speech now referred to as "parentese." Parents the world over of every social standing and in every language have a natural tendency to speak to babies in a higher-pitched, sing-song, melodious voice, emphasizing key vowel sounds.

TEACHING FIRST LANGUAGE

According to Dr. Patricia Kuhl of the University of Washington in Seattle, during the first six months of life babies can distinguish any sound in any language spoken by humans.[58] Adults who have been exposed only to their native language have significant difficulty in perceiving additional languages. The language babies continue to hear will reinforce the neural connections designated for language, while the connections formed and not used regularly will be eliminated.

The exaggerated, clearly pronounced words of parentese provide babies with the building blocks of language and hard wire these building blocks into the brain. To promote language development in your baby during his first six months in his native language, speak clearly in short, simple sentences using plenty of questions and commands. Avoid using questions that ask permission, like "Can Mommy give you a bath?" or "It's time to change your diaper, okay?" (Before long he will be able to say no and mean it.) Name and talk about objects and events that catch his attention. Repeat your sentences to him and imitate the sounds he makes in response. Of course, in order to imitate his response you must pause conversationally, taking turns speaking. Respond as if he communicated. For example, you say, "Mommy's going to change your diaper now." He waves his arms and gurgles. You respond, "Oh, you like that idea? I thought you would." Once he begins saying actual words, continue to use parentese.

WHAT DID HE SAY?

Your toddler points to a tree branch and says, "Booow." You excitedly exclaim, "Bird! He just said 'bird'!" You are convinced and everyone around you says you are blinded by love. Why is his speech so hard to understand, especially to anyone other than his parents?

The parts of his body required for speech are still developing, as is his control over them. He has not yet learned to stop and start his syllables as abruptly as adults or to precisely place his disproportionately large tongue. He knows what he is trying to say and may think he said it. Since he will likely use the same abbreviated sounds, or even substitute sounds, to consistently indicate the same word or words, you may learn his code while everyone else hears only foreign babble.

Be careful not to imitate your baby's mispronunciations, no matter how cute. You want to reinforce the correct way to speak, using "water," rather than "wa-wa." You do not need to correct him every time he says it his way; he will pick up the correct pronunciation by hearing you say it properly. If he says, "Ba-ba!," you can simply say, "Oh! You want your bottle."

Another great way to encourage language development is to read to your baby as often as you can. Reading to him promotes bonding, language development, and reading itself.

To build your child's vocabulary from infancy, emphasize the words you want him to recognize. Repeat the word in parentese several times without using it in a sentence. For example, just before you give him a bath, simply say "baaath" three or four times. Sidney Ledson, author of *Raising Brighter Children*, recommends that you only teach nouns this way, rather than teaching descriptive or action words. He further suggests that you avoid trying to teach words that sound similar within a short period of time (*e.g.*, dog and doll, doll and wall). Also, avoid teaching words within a short period of time that your baby may have trouble distinguishing as separate, such as wall and window, window and glass, fingers and hand, and so on. Use objects that he sees on a daily basis and keep track of the words you emphasize this way.[59]

Get in the habit of explaining *why*. That word will eventually become one of your toddler's favorites, and you want to encourage his desire to reason. Start off with simple, clear explanations when he begins to get around on his own. For example, no matter how well you childproof your home, he will still encounter things that are off limits. Rather than simply saying no, give a simple reason *why* the item is off limits. You could say, "No, that will hurt you. It's hot. Ow!," or you could say, "No, that will break."

HOW BABIES LEARN LANGUAGE

Using magnetic resonance imaging (MRI), scientists have learned much about how humans learn and store language. They have found that newborns encode basic language elements into their brains according to syllables and sounds. They have found by studying bilingual adults that those who learned a second language as babies store that language in the same part of the brain as their native language.

Those adults who learned a second language after adolescence store it in a separate part of the brain, must mentally translate from their native language to the second language, and are not as likely to speak additional languages with a native accent.[60]

TEACHING ADDITIONAL LANGUAGES

To enable your child to speak additional languages, you must expose him to the basic sounds of those languages during his first six months of life. If more than one language is already spoken in your home, designate individuals to use only one language in speaking parentese to him. Studies show that children who hear two languages from one caregiver never learn either language very well. Since babies tend to tune out regular conversation, you may still speak in the dominant language of your household to each other, but have one caregiver use exclusively one additional language when tending to your baby. Some parents have made a financial priority of hiring foreign-language-speaking caregivers for just a few hours a week and instructing them to speak only in their native tongue while caring for the baby. If that is not practical, make use of tapes such as those produced by Sound Beginnings (1-800-460-6802). They offer a tape set developed by linguistic and musical specialists designed to expose your baby to the building blocks of Spanish, French, German, Russian, Hebrew, Japanese, and English. The tapes contain 15-minute sessions in each language set to the music of each culture.

Medically speaking, it should be noted that babies who suffer from chronic middle-ear infections in infancy may fall victim to what is termed "language-based learning disabilities," such as reading problems.[61] Because such a baby never clearly receives auditory signals of certain sounds, he will have difficulty distinguishing between such sounds; the sounds were never hard wired into his brain. Therefore, perceiving the difference in the written word becomes nearly impossible. Therapy in the form of auditory rehabilitation can correct the problem in many cases. Yet an ounce of prevention would certainly be worth a pound of cure in this instance. See that your baby gets regular medical care and especially prompt medical attention when there are symptoms of specific problems.

CHAPTER SUMMARY

Do you remember the following points with regard to your baby's language development?

- The importance of maintaining a running dialogue with your baby;
- The age when babies acquire the ability to use language;
- The importance of "parentese;"
- How to promote your baby's skill development in his native language;
- The pitfalls to avoid;
- How to build your baby's vocabulary;
- The benefits of preparing to explain "why;"
- How to avoid stunting your child's multilingual capabilities; and
- How to develop your baby's multilingual capabilities.

Chapter 9 —
The Sound of Music

As stated previously, the goal of using this program is to give your child every opportunity to reach her full potential in every aspect of her life. You may wonder, however, what music has to do with her intellectual development.

Although music has a direct effect on your baby's intellectual development, you may be interested to know some of the more indirect benefits that exposure to music and musical training have on her overall development. Many of the benefits result from music lessons given after your baby reaches two years of age, but the groundwork you lay in the first two years gives her significant advantages.

Learning to play an instrument requires hours of concentrated effort, which develops your child's perseverance, confidence, discipline, responsibility, and self-esteem. She will gain valuable problem-solving skills as she learns to take what could be an overwhelming task and break it down into manageable steps. Her sense of accomplishment as she conquers each new piece of music gives her the drive to continue for the mere sake of self-improvement and gives her pride in a job well-done. Obviously, because music is an art form, its study develops creativity and self-expression. Your child also learns to follow directions and to work as a team if she plays in an orchestra or band. And, although there are many factors which influence your child's adult life, Dr. Patrick Kavanaugh cited the following very interesting statistics: 1) Over 90% of America's top CEOs and corporate presidents had music lessons in

SING A SONG OF SILLY STUFF

Your infant will love to play with the sound of her own voice and will learn much from yours. Music establishes a foundation for language development and is a wonderful catalyst for bonding. Simple songs will help focus her attention and make it easier for her to learn and remember words. How can you get the most from music?

Keep background music playing. Try singing *The Three Little Pigs* for a change. Make up songs about diaper changing or getting dressed. Turn everyday events into celebrated musicals, using rattles as maracas, buckets as drums, papertowel tubes as flutes, clarinets, or trumpets. Most importantly, have fun together.

their youth; and 2) Over 90% of all criminals on death row did not.[62] These shocking extremes are in no way intended to imply that your baby is headed for a life of crime if she is denied music lessons in childhood; they are, nonetheless, thought-provoking commentaries.

Under the tutelage of world-renowned violin instructor and scholar Dr. Shinichi Suzuki from the time they turn two years of age, four-year-olds leave adults astounded at their incredible performances of classical pieces by Bach and Vivaldi. Baby E.D. pertains to the development of babies up to the age of two, so why is this relevant? Just as your baby begins to learn language(s) from birth, so she begins to learn about music at or before birth.

According to *Newsweek* magazine, researchers at the University of Konstanz in Germany have confirmed the affect of music on your baby's brain circuitry. Through the use of MRIs, they found that more of the brain was dedicated to the thumb and fifth finger of the left hand in children who had been given lessons on stringed instruments. Although the length of time the child practiced each day did not affect the number of connections in the brain, the age at which the child started with the instrument did. The younger the child was when she began, the larger the area of the brain devoted to its use.[63]

According to *Raising Musical Kids*, "music is one of the few activities that uses both the right and left sides of the brain, as well as the mysterious realm 'between' (the *corpus callosum*) that coordinates the two sides."[64] Early exposure to and experimentation with music allows your baby to establish mental pathways she will use throughout her entire life.

Does it matter what type of music your baby hears? Yes. One natural form of music that is especially comforting to newborns is a human heartbeat played at the same level as her mother's heartbeat played in the womb. Although all forms of rock music agitate unborn and newborn babies, most classical and tuneful music soothes and calms them. Brahms and Beethoven have been found to distract newborns, but Bach and Vivaldi have a very soothing effect on them. Listening to Mozart has had an unusually beneficial result: it improves spatial reasoning, which strengthens your baby's ability to comprehend math and logic. Because of the importance of music in your baby's life, some hospitals even receive charitable contributions of selected musical recordings to dispense to newborns and their parents.

Masaru Ibuka, founder of Sony Corporation and author of *Kindergarten Is Too Late!*, cites an example of a couple who played Bach's Suite No. 2 for their newborn a few hours everyday. In three months, the baby was "dancing" to the music, moving her body to the tempo and fussing when the piece finished. The parents were able to use this particular piece to soothe their baby when other methods failed.[65] That benefit alone was worth the effort of playing the music everyday.

In infancy your child is not so much instructed in music as she is exposed to it. Scientists recommend that you play tuneful music two or three hours per day for your baby. Does that seem difficult to fit into your schedule? Use it to signify certain events. For example, when you first get up in the morning, play the music for an hour or so to indicate wake-up time; or play the music for an hour or so before bedtime to indicate settle down time. Starting from infancy will reap huge rewards in later months and years.

Unfortunately, because babies are amazing mimics, they imitate what is bad as well as what is good. This relates to music in that if your baby hears music or singing that is off key or out of tune, her ear for music may be damaged. Since singing to her is another important way to bond with her, you may have to weigh the outcomes if you do not sing well.

Although this program focuses on the development of a child through age two, there are some important things to know when your child does turn two. First, it is during these early years that a child can achieve "absolute pitch," which basically means that she may be able to identify a single note without hearing any other notes around it.

Second, never underestimate what your child can take in. If you are skilled in music and you sit at the piano with her on your lap for ten minutes per day, patiently playing a musical scale while she pounds the keyboard with her fist, you are still providing her with an excellent musical start.

Third, the instrument(s) to which you expose your child should be chosen carefully. A violin is an excellent instrument for a child to learn, but unless a qualified teacher is on hand to correct notes that are being played slightly sharp or slightly flat because of the positioning of the instrument, serious damage can be done to your child's sense of pitch. On the other hand, a piano that is properly tuned produces the correct note simply with the push of the key.

A musical instructor should also be chosen very carefully. Formal training can begin when your child is two years old, but not every music teacher is qualified to teach such a young child. Obviously, the teacher must be patient; but even beyond that, the teaching method makes a difference. If the instructor tries to teach your child to read music before teaching her to play music, your child may lose interest in music altogether. Why? Do you think you would have enjoyed learning to speak if you were taught the parts of speech and sentence structure before you were allowed to express yourself? It is more likely that you learned, and enjoyed learning, by imitating others who spoke to you and around you. It is absolutely vital that your child's interest be kept and her attention stimulated. Some experts even recommend that she be allowed to play in the room with an older sibling or playmate during their lessons, with the teacher's permission of course. Encourage her natural desire to imitate others when there is a good example to be followed. In addition, select a teacher who discerns your child's interest. Is your child more interested in rhythm or harmony, etc.?

Once your baby does reach the age of two, you may benefit by reviewing *Raising Musical Kids*.[66] The book can help you decide which instrument(s) would be best for your toddler to learn. It gives step-by-step instructions for choosing the right music teacher, as well as for instilling a love of music in your child.

CHAPTER SUMMARY

Do you remember the following points with regard to music and your baby's intellectual development?

- The long-term impact of musical groundwork laid in the first two years;
- The affect of music on your baby's brain and its development;
- The benefits of exposing your baby to particular types of music;
- How to expose your baby to music;
- The importance of instrument selection;
- The importance of carefully selecting a musical instructor; and
- Where to turn for additional information after your baby reaches the age of two.

Chapter 10 — Help Your Baby Read All about It

Any parent will tell you that children learn what you do much faster than they learn what you tell them. So, read to your newborn! Hold him close in your lap, and read to him while he feels close and secure and loved. He will associate reading with a pleasant, joyful experience and look forward to doing it for himself one day. But when?

Many parents associate the task of teaching a child to read with the early years of school. Yet, why help your child learn to speak and then wait four or five years before helping him learn to read? As soon as he can grasp that words represent objects, he can grasp that written symbols represent words. Studies show that the earlier a child learns to read, the better his future academic performance. The *Journal of Developmental and Behavioral Pediatrics* noted a significant link between age and reading ability. The study found that children who started school later were more likely to be poor readers than children who started kindergarten at the "normal" age.[67] This underscores the importance of starting your baby's reading program during the toddler/preschool years, since each passing year decreases his optimum reading capacity.

HOW TO READ TO YOUR BABY

The Positions. Hold your newborn close in your arms, and snuggle while reading. It does not matter if she is looking at the book or even seems aware that you are reading. As she starts getting around on her own, you can still hold her to read; but be ready to keep the reading short. Five minutes may be an eternity to an exploring baby. When she becomes a toddler, try laying on the floor reading the stories aloud for yourself and invite her to join in.

The Drama. Make the stories live! Perform the stories with your voice. Point out interesting elements of the pictures. Make the experience fun.

The Technique. Point to the words on the page as you say them. Help her follow along.

Actually, just talking to your child is the beginning of teaching him to read. He must first comprehend that words have meaning before reading will mean anything to him. Yet, even before he comprehends the meanings of words, you can begin teaching him by providing him with brightly colored alphabet toys and referring to them by name. Start with one or two and gradually add others. Never try to push your child to read. Keep it simple, keep it interesting, make it fun. Be aware of his attention span and try to change the subject before he becomes bored. By the time he begins to walk, he may be able to identify most or all of the letters, although he will not yet grasp their purpose.

According to I Am Your Child, an organization aimed at enriching the lives of children, studies show that *the way* you read to your baby makes a difference.

> "Read stories in a way that encourages older babies and toddlers to participate — by answering your questions, by pointing out what they see in a picture book, by telling you what they think will happen next in the story, and by repeating rhymes and refrains. Telling the same stories and singing the same songs over and over may feel boring to you, but not to children. They learn through repetition. And that doesn't only apply to language."[68]

Experts also recommend that, from the beginning, you point to the words as you read them. Doing so eventually acquaints your baby with two principles: 1) those little black marks on the page have meaning, and 2) reading in English is done from left to right.

Author Vicki Lansky recommends telling stories to your baby to encourage interest in reading. If you are not a naturally creative storyteller, fear not. The following suggestions may not make you Hans Christian Anderson, but you can get your own creative juices flowing well enough to make a story come to life. First, all good stories start with "Once upon a time ..." Next, pull your story's characters from your baby's world: family members, family pets, toys, trees, planets, the bath tub faucet, or anything around you. Give the main character(s) a

WHAT TO READ TO YOUR BABY AND WHEN

You can start before she is born or you can start right after. In the first four months, it does not matter what you read. The important thing is the togetherness. Gradually introduce picture books with simple phrases or rhymes. Start with talking about the pictures, and as she gets older emphasize the story using varied voices for characters. Once your baby is talking, ask her questions about the story and the characters in it. Have her fill in rhyming words at the end of the sentence.

goal and keep it lively. You should have something exciting happen right away and keep the story moving along. Do not worry about whether you are using words that are too complicated for him; just be sure to give the story a happy ending. Realism is definitely not a required part of a fairy tale![69]

The preceding paragraphs discuss vital steps that are most beneficial when started at (or before) birth. Even though some children with very involved parents can learn to read before they can even speak,* reading programs typically begin when the child is around two years old. When your toddler reaches the age of two, you may want to do a great deal of research before selecting a program for teaching him to read. There are quite a number of theories on the *best* way to teach a child to read, and the subject is hotly debated by experts of equally impressive credentials.

One program promoted by Sidney Ledson, author of *Teach Your Child to Read in 60 Days*, involves a method he used to teach his daughter to read before the age of three. He strongly discourages the teaching of letter names to toddlers (including the singing of their ABCs) because their limited vocabulary will make it difficult for them to comprehend the difference between phonics (letter sounds) and letter names. If your toddler already knows his ABCs, Ledson states that you can then try to illustrate the difference by explaining the difference between your family pet's name and the sound that pet makes.[70] That does seem like a rather involved concept to expect an 18-month-old child to comprehend. Nevertheless, if science has learned anything about baby's minds, it is that they should *never* be underestimated!

HOW TO START TEACHING YOUR BABY TO READ IN THE FIRST TWO YEARS

1. Talk to him.
2. Sing to him.
3. Read to him.
4. Tell him stories.
5. Turn letters and books into toys.
6. Let him see you reading.

---

* Such children indicate by gestures that they recognize the words they are reading. Intellectual development and physical development are entirely different. Physical development usually comes at its own pace, barring neglect or abuse. Since physical development includes the ability to control the muscles of the lips, tongue, mouth, and vocal cords for speech, your baby may be intellectually ready to speak long before he is physically able to do so.

Another program declares that learning the names of the letters is the first step in learning to read.[71] Yet another program cites the study of Einstein's brain. That program claims that Einstein's brain was found to be more similar to a preschooler's brain than to an adult brain. They believe this indicates that Einstein continued to learn as children learn, with his senses rather than through rote memorization of facts. As soon as children begin to attend traditional schools, they are broken from the "natural" form of learning and forced into the "unnatural" form of cramming facts. Therefore, that program believes that children should be taught to read through visual mapping, actually training them to maintain photographic memories. The implications of that are enormous when you consider what other capacities that makes possible.

Dr. Thomas Armstrong warns that reading programs which include flashcards and other equipment typical of a preschool or elementary school classroom "may actually confuse infants or create stress that can block, not promote, new learning." The reason for this is that babies learn through their bodies and through active exchanges with the physical world around them. Since flashcards and similar materials have little or nothing to do with the real world, their effect can be counterproductive. When infants do respond to these flashcards, it may be more an example of conditioned responses and modified behavior, than a true learning or building of mental pathways for future use. Dr. Armstrong recommends that you concentrate instead on developmentally appropriate experiences, such as "singing, talking, hugging and holding, and lots of concrete materials."[72] For examples of such concrete materials, refer to the age-appropriate sections of Baby E.D.'s Educational Play chapters.

These are just a few examples of the theories currently propounded in teaching children to read. In any case, you would do well to investigate as many of these theories as possible and then make an informed decision for yourself on what you believe to be in your child's best interest. There is no reason, however, to become overwhelmed with the possibilities and simply resign to leaving the teaching of reading to the schools. The experts *do* agree on the fact that learning to read during the toddler years is extremely beneficial to your child's future. They also agree that the foundation you lay during the first two years is critical to helping your child to read as a toddler. So, keep talking to him and keep reading to him following the suggestions in the beginning of this chapter.

CHAPTER SUMMARY

Do you remember the following points with regard to reading and your baby's intellectual development?

- How to start your newborn on the road to reading;
- The age at which children should be taught to read;
- The pitfalls to avoid;
- The controversy over the different methods of teaching babies to read;
- The most effective way to read to your baby;
- How to make up and tell a story; and
- Researching teaching methods for children over the age of two.

Chapter 11 — Is Your Little Calculator Ready for Math?

Teaching your baby math, like teaching your baby to read, raises strong emotions from child care professionals on both sides of the issue. Interestingly, though, math exposure has something else in common with reading exposure. As some experts believe your baby should learn to read before learning her ABCs, so too some experts believe she should learn to perform math exercises before learning to recognize the symbols used to represent quantities: the 1-2-3s. Babies can perceive quantities without knowing the symbol that represents each quantity, and they can add and subtract quantities as well. For example, if your baby sees three bananas and you take two away, she will recognize the difference.

BABY MATH

Your baby may not be ready to balance your checkbook, but she is already a natural at working on the basics. As a newborn, she can clearly recognize the differences between various shapes, like circles, squares, and triangles. She can also recognize quantities long before she can identify numbers. In fact, your little investigator will spend a great deal of time sorting her world into categories using the concepts of geometry, one-to-one correspondence, greater than, less than, larger, smaller, and so on. You can encourage this process by talking about everyday things: "One shoe, two shoes. Two shoes! One foot, two feet. Two feet! One foot goes in one shoe. The other foot goes in the other shoe. Two feet. Two shoes. Hurray!"

As she grows, she will begin to successfully nest a half-cup measuring cup into a three-quarter-cup measuring cup, fit one end of a square into the end of another square, put a triangle through the triangle opening of a shape sorter, and piece together large puzzle pieces. The thrill each accomplishment brings will foster a greater love for learning and achieving.

At least one expert espouses the practice of teaching your baby math as young as eight months old.[73] However, due to the criticism of that expert's work and the lack of recent information on the subject, Baby E.D. leaves this subject to the parents' discretion. Should you decide to further investigate the issue for your child, the following information is provided: Author Glen Doman, founder of the Institute for the Advancement of Human Potential, has a series of books that teach babies academic skills with the use of flashcards (*e.g.*, *Teach Your Baby to Read,*[74] *Teach Your Baby Math*,[75] etc.). Author Burton L. White speaks against this method of teaching and specifically against Doman's work in his book *The New First Three Years of Life*.[76]

CHAPTER SUMMARY

Do you remember the following topics with regard to math skills and your baby's intellectual development?

- The controversy on teaching your baby math skills; and
- Additional sources for parental research on the matter.

PART II: AGE-SPECIFIC ACTIVITIES

Chapter 12 — Educational Play for the First Twenty-Four Months

Exposing your baby to different intellectual stimuli is one way to enrich his development. Another very successful way to help him learn and grow is through intellectual play. Learning should be fun and exciting for him. The more he enjoys learning, the more likely he is to make it a lifelong pursuit.

While there are many books and programs written on educational play, the following chapters are based on concepts presented by Dr. S. H. Jacob in his book *Your Baby's Mind*.[77] His emphasis is on age-specific learning based on the child development theories of Jean Piaget. Of course, the activities and toys described in these chapters are merely suggestions of the types of activities and toys

MOTOR SKILL DEVELOPMENT: HANDLING A RATTLE

Your baby may spend a month or two on each step before moving on to the next.

Step 1. Your baby will grip a rattle placed in his hand.

Step 2. His grip will loosen and he will be better able to maneuver the rattle.

Step 3. He will flail the rattle over his body and become aware of the connection between the movement and the noise.

Step 4. Staring at his fingers in amazement, he will grab the rattle for himself.

Step 5. Working on his eye-hand coordination, he will reach for the rattle, grab it, and inspect it with his eyes and mouth.

Step 6. He will practice grabbing the rattle with a "pincer grasp" using his thumb and index finger like tweezers.

Step 7. He will start passing the rattle from one hand to the other and rotating his wrists as he waves the rattle in the air.

Step 8. By now, he will probably be sitting up on his own and using both hands to reach for, grab, bang, shake, and poke the rattle.

Step 9. Still working towards precision, he will enjoy the separate use of his fingers, poking his index finger through the handle.

Step 10. Now able to curl and uncurl his fingers, he will love to grab, drop, and fling the rattle over and over again.

beneficial at each stage of your baby's development. You are encouraged to be creative in expanding on these suggestions. Remember to smile and keep a running dialogue with him, describing everything you do together. These activities should be incorporated throughout his day in addition to the information presented in the previous chapters of this book.

BENEFITS OF PLAY

Playing is an important part of your baby's intellectual development. In infancy, playing mainly benefits the development of his motor skills and senses. Since he begins intellectual development through motor-sensory experiences, playing is vital in early months. Physical play improves his flexibility and also develops his emotions; he learns to distinguish your reactions, take turns, and control his own emotions and activities. By playing, he develops necessary thought processes, such as perceiving order and sequencing, laying down neural paths for future use. Furthermore, playing with you increases his vocabulary, concentration, and patience. Playing with simple toys helps him enjoy the "journey" as much as reaching the destination, thus lessening or delaying his desire for instant gratification.

NO BABY IS AN ISLAND

Your baby needs time to play by himself for a number of reasons: to learn to entertain himself, to explore and discover at his own pace, and to build a sense of independence. Yet playing alone does not mean being isolated from other people.

When your baby is only two months old, he can tell the difference between language directed at him and language directed at others. If you allow him to play in the room where you are, he will continue to learn from you while he is playing by himself. How? He will pick up on the rhythm of conversation even though he is focused on his activity.

While you want to encourage independent play, you do not want to force it on him. If he wants your attention, you will do more harm than good if you force him to play alone.

Imaginative play teaches your baby compassion and empathy as he learns to see things through the eyes of others. Such play also fosters creativity that can find later expression in any number of fields: art, sculpture, music, writing, social skills, public speaking, etc. Each of these benefits directly and indirectly affect his intellectual growth.

CREATIVITY

The book *Toys, Play, and Child Development* by Cambridge University listed the following seven suggestions for encouraging creativity in toddlers:[78]

1. Tell stories to your baby.

2. Read stories to your baby.

3. Initiate pretend play with your baby.

4. Provide a place or allow the use of a place your baby selects for make believe (*e.g.*, a safe corner of the kitchen or dining room while you are in those areas).

5. View your child's make-believe play as healthy and beneficial, rather than viewing it as annoying nonsense or fearing insanity or "weirdness."

6. Prevent older children's ridiculing your baby's active imagination.

7. Provide your toddler with simpler playthings (*e.g.*, scrap paper, paints, molding clay or dough, wooden blocks, cardboard cartons, pipe cleaners, rag dolls, and costumes) that allow room for imagination, rather than structured toys (*e.g.*, name-brand dolls with specific outfits, doll houses or miniature service stations, plastic molds and cutters for clay and dough, and elaborately constructed toys).

Surprisingly, the older your toddler is, the simpler his toys should be. As his ability to imagine grows, his toys should allow for more imagination; whereas while he is younger, he will need replicas of everyday objects (*e.g.*, cars, phones, people, etc.) to begin imaginative play.

In general, you should not need to spend much money on toys. The simplest household objects are often favorite playthings: wooden spoons, empty oatmeal boxes, plastic bowls, laundry baskets, and you. However, when you do purchase toys, you may enjoy those available from *Parents* magazine's Child Development

Toys program. The toys are specifically designed for encouraging reaching, grabbing, exploring, chewing, and rolling. They provide visual, auditory, and textile stimulation without overdoing it. They help develop eye-hand coordination and the discovery of cause and effect. Each toy also comes with an informative Play & Learning Guide, from which some of Baby E.D.'s information was taken.

Chapter 13 — Birth to One Month

Human infants are more dependent on their parents and caregivers than any other animal species. What an opportunity for you to make a difference in your child's life! According to Dr. S. H. Jacob, misconceptions of babies' capabilities cause some parents to have such low expectations that they "simply do not bother to offer any special enrichment. Consequently, they miss out on the joys that come with serving and aiding their child's earliest development."[79] He further states that parents' providing just "bodily" care results in depriving babies "of the significant early enrichment that can mean so much intellectually later in life." Fortunately for your baby, you have no intention of making those mistakes!

Despite what myths you may have heard, your baby at birth has a fully developed sense of smell, taste, and hearing. Her sight is limited, however. She can focus best on objects around seven to ten inches in front of her, and she can perceive depth as well as shapes and patterns of color, contrast, and contour. Her staring into space may actually constitute a state of heightened awareness in which she is taking in information from her environment with all her senses; therefore, do not feel compelled to snap her out of it. She can also pay attention to things seen or heard that capture her notice. However, she does not yet comprehend that objects exist separate from herself.

THAT FACE!

Psychologist R. L. Fantz tested the visual interest of forty-nine infants from the ages of four days old to six months old by showing them a number of test objects. The object that stimulated the greatest interest in every age level: a frontal view of the human face! Dr. Fantz determined: "Innate knowledge of the environment is demonstrated ... by the interest of young infants in kinds of form that will later aid in object recognition, social responsiveness and spatial orientation."[80]

Many feel that visual stimulation and toys are of no use during the first four weeks of life. While that may be true, the same experts strongly emphasize the importance of bonding and parent-child interchanges during the first month. They also acknowledge that babies demonstrate a growing interest in visual stimulation and toys toward the end of the first month.

Between birth and one month, your baby is mainly reactive, responding to things, events, and feelings, rather than initiating responses. She has just come from a very comfortable, secure, regulated environment into a wide open world where nearly everything is new to her. Allow her to adjust to this new environment and encourage her to enjoy the many benefits of life on the outside.

THAT POWERFUL SMILE

There is not a tooth in her mouth, but her smile can melt you like butter in the mid-August sun. Then a jealous by-stander says, "She's probably just got gas."

The truth is, early smiles are more a result of an immature nervous system than of social graces. Nevertheless, they draw you in heart first. So, when does she smile because she likes you, and how do you know she is not just imitating your smile?

Somewhere between three and five weeks of age, she will begin to smile at the sight of you. This is no act of imitation. She has no idea what her face looks like when she smiles. Blind babies do the same thing. Your baby's smile is an outward reflection of the happy warmth she feels within.

The decorations, toys, and activities recommended in this section help: first, to stimulate your baby's senses to increase brain activity and strengthen the connections necessary for sight, hearing, and the other senses; second, to exercise her reflexes.

Your baby learns about her new environment through the use of certain reflexes with which she was born: grasping, sucking, blinking, rooting, and so on. For example, when you put your finger in the palm of her hand and she grabs it, she learns about your finger's temperature, texture, and size. During her first month you want to help her exercise these reflexes to prepare her for the next stage in development, which is to combine these reflexes to learn even more about the world around her. Until then, remember that she has no concept of objects existing separate from herself. She also does not yet realize that objects continue to exist when out of her sight.

Since your purpose in stimulating your baby's intellect is to enrich her development, you will want to be careful not to try to hurry her growth. Instead, provide a loving, warm environment of guided play in which she feels relaxed and happy. If you are overdoing things, she will let you know by shutting you out and going to sleep. This self-defense mechanism protects her from over-stimulation and alerts you to her limitations. As she grows, she will tolerate more and more stimulation until she reaches a point at which you wonder if you can ever do enough to satisfy her intellectual hunger. In the meantime, take advantage of this opportunity to learn her temperament and the signals she uses to express herself.

> **COLOR MY WORLD**
>
> It probably comes as no surprise that color influences people's moods. Hospitals, mental institutions, and day-care centers have benefitted from that information for years now. You may be surprised, however, to learn that color even influences I.Q. scores in children. According to Sidney Ledson in *Raising Brighter Children,* a three-year study in Germany resulted in just that inescapable conclusion. Children whose I.Q.s were tested in rooms the children considered to be beautiful or even in their favorite color (yellow, yellow-green, orange, or light blue) actually scored an average of as much as 12 points higher. When tested in rooms the children considered to be of an ugly color (white, black, brown), the children's scores dropped by an average of 14 points.
>
> Further, the children who were allowed to play in the beautifully colored rooms with beautifully colored toys for 18 months scored 25 points higher than those who played in traditional kindergarten settings for the same period of time. The children in the rooms they considered beautiful were found to be more alert, more creative, 53% friendlier, less irritable, and 12% less hostile.
>
> Ledson suggests that if painting your baby's room in happy colors is not an option, perhaps you can paint and decorate large, flattened cardboard boxes and use them as wall hangings.[81]

DECORATIONS/ MOBILES

Select sheets, blankets, and cribside padding with bright contrasting colors and simple designs, preferably including even abstract drawings of the human face. Lamaze offers an excellent play quilt and cribside graphic panels in its Infant Development System, but you can also make your own. Likewise, choose or make a cribside banner of solid-color fabric with a variety of shapes cut out of various colors and types of fabric attached to it.

You can easily make a mobile by securely fastening a ribbon or length of elastic across the top of your baby's crib with soft, light, safe objects dangling from it: a baby spoon, a piece of colorful cloth, a rattle, a baby toy. If you buy a mobile, be sure to choose one that has an interesting view from her angle. Many experts recommend that, during

your baby's first two months, you should hang simple mobiles (*e.g.*, a shoe box with cut-outs of human faces pasted to it) on the side of her crib. She will probably spend most of her crib time either on her side or on her back with her head turned to one side during the first two months. Be sure to remove these items before she is old enough to actually pull on them.

TOYS

Because the human face is so stimulating to a newborn, buy or make a hand puppet with a human face. Other great toys include:

- your fingers,
- plastic measuring spoons/cups,
- wash cloths,
- large plastic rings,
- large wooden spoons, and
- nearly anything that cannot be swallowed and will not hurt your baby if it drops on her head.

ACTIVITIES

Remember to take turns talking to your baby, allowing time for her response to what you say. Use a warm, loving voice.

❑

Sing lullabies and nursery rhymes to your baby.

❑

Read to her. Include her when you go about your daily routine by reading everything out loud, such as recipes, instructions, and articles you read for yourself.

❑

Play tuneful music for her, especially classical music from Vivaldi, Bach, and Mozart.

❑

Massage your baby, for about fifteen minutes every day. She will especially enjoy a massage when she wakes up from a nap or after a warm bath.

❑

Touch your baby's cheek with various objects, such as your hand, the satin edge of a blanket, a sweater, a rattle, a rubber ball, a soft toy, etc. This activity will make her familiar with different textures.

Chapter 14 —
One to Four Months

At this age your baby's discoveries will start accidentally and will generally be limited to distinguishing parts of his body. He will begin to realize that he can exercise the reflexes with which he was born voluntarily. Encourage this exercise and the discovering of his body parts. Remember that baby learning involves using all the senses, including taste. Thus, his sucking his hand, thumb, and toes is a sign of intellectual growth, despite how it may appear to adults.

Your baby will accidentally cause a reaction and will try to repeat the action to obtain the same reaction. Perhaps his arm jerks while he is holding the rattle you put in his hand. He will work hard to learn how to move his arm on purpose to make the noise again. Because he will begin to initiate actions on his own, he will begin to play and imitate. His coordination will be improving as he begins intentionally creating and repeating his own motions. This is all due to his beginning to combine and coordinate individual reflex actions into whole action patterns. For instance, the startle reflex includes your baby's arms jerking up toward his face. The sucking reflex allows him to suck something that you put in his mouth. (In the womb he could suck his thumb only if his hand floated up close enough to his mouth.) Now he can deliberately move his arm upward, bring his hand to his mouth, and suck his thumb. This is an important step in his development as it leads to the next stage: learning to manipulate objects in the world around him. That opens up entirely new categories of information.

I CAN SEE WITH MY MOUTH!

Just how much does your baby learn by putting an object in his mouth? Researchers found out by testing four-month-olds. The researchers gave one group of babies smooth pacifiers and another group nubby pacifiers, without letting the babies see either type of pacifier. Later, when the babies were shown both types of pacifiers, the babies who sucked smooth pacifiers were more interested in looking at the smooth pacifier. Babies who sucked nubby pacifiers, were more interested in looking at the nubby pacifier.[82]

This second stage (one to four months of age) also marks another important development in human intellect, that of accommodations. Your baby becomes less helpless as he learns to adjust his own body position to be more comfortable and as he learns to change his grip on a toy according to its shape. While this may seem a small beginning, it actually portrays profound mental growth in his ability to adjust to fit the demands of new circumstances.

Your baby's memory is also developing. It is at the very earliest stages of allowing him to form simple mental images, the type that allow him to recognize you, for example. He is developing the concept of objects, beginning to understand what things are, and building his database of information on these objects. This is a vital foundation since future discoveries will be compared to what your baby already considers familiar, relating information by comparison.

DECORATIONS/MOBILES

The items described in the previous chapter are still best for your baby's intellectual stimulation through this stage as well. However, you can change the objects suspended from the mobile periodically to allow him to experience as much variety as possible. Also, for the period between three and nine weeks of age, you can suspend pictures of human faces pasted to sheets of cardboard in the form of a mobile approximately 10 to 12 inches from the side of your baby's face. Use brightly colored yarn or string to hang the pictures. The mobile need not be very sturdy since your baby will not be reaching for it or grabbing it at this age.

At two to three months of age, your baby can gradually see up to a distance of two feet. He will still prefer human adult and baby faces to nearly any other object, and he will be better able to make eye contact. He will also become more skilled at differentiating between details of colors and features.

I SEE WHAT YOU'RE SAYING

Studies have shown that not only do infants distinguish language from other sounds, they can match speech with the speaker!

One study played an audio tape with a person speaking while the infants watched two screens, each with a person speaking. After looking back and forth between the two screens, every baby focused on the face that matched the sounds they were hearing.[83]

At three to four months of age, your baby can see up to three feet in front of him and will now begin to take interest in smaller toys and detailed images, as well as various mobiles and movement.

TOYS

In addition to the toys listed in Chapter 13, you can now add the following and similar toys:

- your face,
- his face (an unbreakable mirror will give him access to that),
- wooden blocks,
- plastic blocks,
- different rattles and teethers,
- balls of various materials,
- stuffed animals/dolls with large faces,
- plastic rings, and
- an aluminum pie plate, etc.

ACTIVITIES

In addition to the activities previously described, present your baby with a variety of textures from various types of fabric and toys for his discovery. Remember to look into his eyes, smile, and echo his attempts at vocal communication.

❑

Allow your baby to exercise his grasp by brushing objects across his fingers until he grabs it. Be careful not to irritate or frustrate him, though. Success will encourage more attempts.

❑

Place his hands on his cheeks and then on your cheeks; on his nose and then on your nose; etc. Describe what you are doing. For example:

"Jessie's cheeks, Mommy's cheeks. Oooh, soft cheeks. That feels nice, doesn't it?"

❑

Make pleasant faces of varied expressions while slowly bobbing your head from one area of his vision to another.

❑

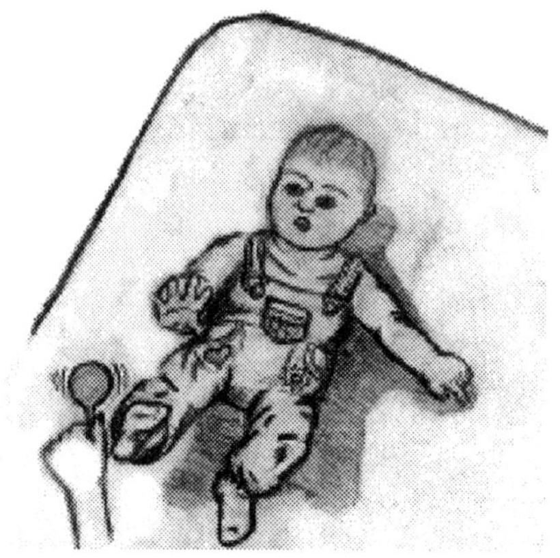

With your baby on his back, gently shake a rattle above his head, then off to the left of his ankles, then to the right of his shoulders, and so on, allowing him to follow the rattle with his eyes.

❑

Now turn your baby over onto his stomach. Help him strengthen his neck by slowly lifting toys in front of his face while he raises his head to follow them.

❑

Wear your baby around the house and while running errands. Talk about the sights, sounds, and smells. Remember that if he turns his head, goes to sleep, or starts to cry, he has had enough; he needs a break.

❑

Bounce the light from a flashlight around a fairly dark room, allowing him to follow the light with his eyes.

❑

With common sense precautions, tie a colorful ribbon or piece of yarn loosely around his wrist or ankle to catch his attention as he flails his arms and legs.

❑

Place a colorful sock on your baby's hand, if it does not irritate or frustrate him. Lamaze has an excellent pair of "Foot Finders" that can help him discover his feet and hands.

❑

Hold your baby upright in a standing position for a few minutes. Changing positions gives him a different perspective on things.

❑

Play pat-a-cake.

❑

Expose your baby to a variety of non-startling noises from different points around him, such as humming, making clicking sounds, using sound-producing toys, and making ordinary household sounds in his presence: vacuuming; ringing the doorbell; moving dishes, pots, and pans; and allowing him to hear pet sounds.

❑

Play peek-a-boo with your face; play peek-a-boo with small toys (rattles, teething rings, etc.) by covering and uncovering them in your baby's sight.

❑

When your baby starts to imitate your sounds, sing a musical scale (if you can do so well).

Chapter 15 — Four to Eight Months

This is a very exciting stage in your baby's development. During this stage, she is beginning actual thought processes that involve intentions. She is beginning to understand cause and effect, along with finding means to an end. The process begins with her accidentally producing an interesting outcome. When she realizes that what he did actually caused the outcome, she repeats the action to continue to produce the same result. Although this process started during the last stage in body-oriented learning, it has now progressed to objects outside her body. Note, though, that this is just the beginning of intentional actions. She accidentally discovers an outcome rather than conceiving of a goal and then devising a plan to accomplish that goal. The activities suggested in this chapter help her "stumble" into this process so that she can fine-tune this new form of thinking and be better prepared to move into fully intentional goal setting and achievement.

MOTOR SKILL DEVELOPMENT: BECOMING MOBILE

From birth to two years of age, big changes take place in your baby's ability to move around. Here is the general order of steps she will take. (Her health care practitioner can tell you if she is on schedule for her age.)

Step 1. Your baby will start to push herself over, usually from stomach to back first.

Step 2. She may move like an inch worm, scooting around without actually crawling.

Step 3. She will practice pushing up on wobbly arms and legs.

Step 4. She will begin to actually move around on all fours, probably in unpredictable directions starting with reverse.

Step 5. Once she learns to crawl forward, she may dart around at near lightening speed.

Step 6. By the time she is able to crawl, she will try to climb on nearly anything that has more than one level.

Step 7. Along with climbing comes standing and cruising. She will pull herself up and walk around the furniture, holding on with one or both hands.

Step 8. As her skill improves she will venture out a few steps at a time.

Step 9. Look, Ma! No hands!

Your baby is becoming mobile and you may feel she has grown as many hands as an octopus has tentacles. All the exploring previously done with the mouth (which will reach its peak around five months of age) will be increasingly performed with seemingly omnipresent little hands. Safety now extends beyond toys to the rest of the house. Provide a clean, safe crawl area, free from electrical cords, open electrical outlets, household chemicals and cleaners, drugs, open stairs, objects small enough to swallow, and sharp objects.

Besides extending her range of exploration, your baby will now begin making more noise than she has before. She will begin to discover that she can actually affect the objects around her, a discovery process you want to encourage. Keeping the benefit to her in mind will help you endure the noise. It will also help you endure the repetition of activities that become tedious to adults and of which babies never seem to tire.

WHO'S THE BEST PLAYMATE?

Researchers have found definite benefits to children playing by themselves. The younger the child is, however, the more she will need an adult to help get the play started. After all, adults provide ideas, toys, and activities when a newborn cannot yet initiate play.

Besides independent play and play with adults, babies and toddlers also benefit from playing with older children. While parents patiently and lovingly help their baby to make new discoveries, older children are interested purely in the play itself. Your baby or toddler can be much inspired by the older child's spirit of play, being immersed in the world of pretend. She would be happy to be the older child's understudy. Because the older child would not be as accommodating as you are, your baby or toddler would stretch to keep up. She would learn valuable social skills such as negotiating through tension and handling frustration.

So should your child play by herself, with you, or with older children? All three types of play are important to her enriched development.

Babies begin to exercise a measure of independence around four to six months of age, presenting a new challenge to parents: balance! Up to this point you have done everything for your infant. Now, however, you must resist the urge to keep her an infant. When she tries to hold a bottle for herself, let her. When she reaches for a rattle that is just out of her range, leave it where it is. Encourage her to work at getting it for herself. When she is no longer content to be in your arms most of her waking hours, see that as positive evidence of growth and maturing. Allow her to crawl, even if it is *away* from you. While you should still gladly lavish love and affection on her (all of her life), you must be more aware of what she considers smothering. Like all of us, babies need space. Pay attention to her signals. If she becomes fussy or seems frustrated, it may be time to back off a little. She should always know that you are there for her when she really needs you, but she should be allowed and encouraged to explore her independence. After all, a major part of your job as parent is to prepare her to lead a successful, happy life on her own, enabling her to share her special gifts and talents with others.

Even though your baby is becoming more independent of you physically, she is still very dependent on you emotionally. *Advances in Infancy Research, Volume 6,* states that, in order to compensate for the loss of physical closeness to you, she will develop a form of social referencing. This means that she will "search for emotional information from the face, voice, or gesture" of the people she trusts.[84] Your vocal, facial, or bodily reaction to her activities wields much influence over her. What does this mean for you? You must be around to give her the feedback she needs. She may seem to be moving away from you, but she will frequently be looking over her shoulder for your guidance.

At four months of age, your baby is able to distinguish emotional reactions in your face: surprise, joy, anger, fear, and neutral expressions. Try to keep that in mind when supervising her explorations. Now she not only recognizes these expressions, she seeks information in them, especially when she encounters new and unfamiliar situations. While some people may feel that they can fool a baby by using a calm, sweet voice although they are quite distressed, the evidence shows that the baby reads facial expressions, as well as vocal expressions and body language. If your baby stops your heart from beating as she reaches for a dangerous object, you should allow your fear to find expression in your face and voice as you jump to her rescue. Such information will impress on her the danger of the situation, rather than confusing her with a calm, "No, no, no" as your eyes bulge in their sockets. In situations where you specifically prefer not to make a big deal of something, be consistent with non-chalance in face, voice, and body. If she has discovered how to spit and you prefer that she did not practice this particular skill, you may choose to ignore it and hope the behavior will go away. Whether you choose to scrunch up your face in disgust or not is up to you. Just be aware that, even though she is just an infant, she knows what your reaction means.

DECORATIONS/MOBILES

At four to six months of age, your baby can see across the room and distinguish different shades of the same color. At six to nine months she can see a distance of nearly 20 feet, and she will start to cry her first real tears. Realizing the effect she can have on objects in her world, she will begin repeating actions to produce the same outcome to her own amazement and delight. Share her delight, and encourage this discovery. One way to do so is by installing new decorations and mobiles in her crib. Hang rattles, bells, chimes, colorful balls, and similar items along the railing of her crib to give her more opportunities to accidentally cause a reaction that catches her attention.

Make a kickboard at the foot of your baby's crib with bells attached and place him close enough to kick the board.

Dangle a kickable mobile across the middle of your baby's crib or play pen.

TOYS

Your baby will be working hard on her hand-eye coordination, and it is a good time to start playing peek-a-boo games and providing her with sorters, blocks, and windup toys.

Any toys you may have used before can still be used if they are sturdy enough to withstand more intensive play. Many commercially available toys are marked with age recommendations. Follow those recommendations carefully. Keeping in mind that almost every toy goes into your baby's mouth at one time or another, please wash the toys before you give them to her. Now is also a good time to introduce the following items and similar toys or activity centers:

- pinwheels,
- pop up toys,
- toys that can be grabbed with one hand,
- toys with smooth, round edges,
- toys with no detachable parts,
- toys that can withstand chewing, pinching, dropping, and throwing,
- noise-making toys, and
- toys with moving parts.

THE WORD ON WALKERS

Walkers have received much attention in the last few years. The number of emergency room visits caused by walker accidents prompted stricter guidelines for manufacturers and the call from at least one organization for a ban on their use. Now many walkers are more like suspension chairs in an activity ring and some are like small push carts. Outside of the safety issues, recent studies have been done on other effects of walker use.

The results of the studies suggest that babies who use walkers that block a view of their feet usually walk around one month later than babies who do not use walkers. Babies who can see their feet in their walkers are only delayed in walking by a couple of weeks.

Since babies generally start walking anywhere between nine and eighteen months anyway, this may not be an issue to you. What should be of interest, though, is that researchers now believe that walkers and stationery exercise saucers cause physical and mental developmental delays. Babies who must crawl to get around have more one-on-one contact with their environment. This increased exposure naturally increases their knowledge of the world around them in a way walker use cannot.[85]

ACTIVITIES

Music, reading, singing, language tapes, and talking are still very important parts of your baby's everyday life. In addition, try incorporating one or more of the following activities into each day.

❑

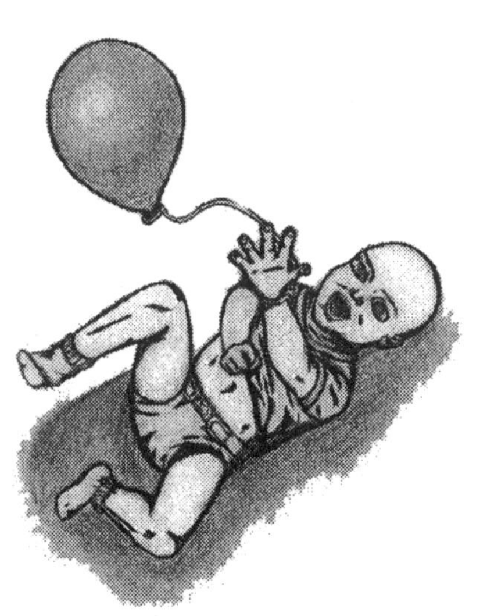

Loosely tie a helium balloon around your baby's ankle or wrist and allow her to discover the effect her movements have on the balloon. Do not leave her unattended with the balloon or string.

❑

Attach a wrist rattle to your baby's wrist or make one by tying bells or a colorful ball of yarn around her wrist. This activity also requires your close supervision.

❑

Sew bells onto a colorful piece of cloth for your baby to shake and toss while you look on.

❑

Attach a noisy toy, such as a tambourine, to a string and hand the other end of the string to your baby to tug. Switch the noisy object with a silent but active object, meaning a toy with lots of moving parts.

❑

Splashing water during bathtime is an exciting science lesson in making everything from small ripples to noisy and surprising splashes. (Be careful of water on the floor when taking her out of the tub.)

❑

When your baby is sitting up on his own, suspend noise-making objects and colorful toys or safe household objects over his head where he can swat them with his hands.

❑

Seat your baby on the floor with a collection of non-breakable pots and a wooden spoon. She will love it, and you will love her enough to endure the noise.

❑

Sit on the floor with your baby and roll a ball back and forth between you.

❑

Fill your cheeks with air and use your baby's hands to squeeze the air back out of them over and over again.

❑

Gently hold your baby's hand to your mouth while you make silly sounds.

❑

Seat your baby with a set of stacking or nesting toys (toys that fit inside each other), bowls, or lightweight pots. Put them together and then take them apart in front of her as a demonstration. Then, let her do whatever she wants with them. Do not expect her to perform any specific assignment.

❑

In previous months you brushed rattles and fabrics against your baby's hands to encourage her grasping reflex. Now, with your baby on her back, do the same with her feet to encourage her continued gain of control over her leg muscles and eye-foot coordination.

❑

Reintroduce old toys in a new way. For example, attach a bell to a squeaky toy or change the clothes on a doll or puppet.

❑

Introduce different textures and masses, like wooden blocks, plastic stacking donuts, and furry stuffed animals. Always describe the things that attract your baby's attention.

❑

Your baby will be developing the concept of object permanence during this time period. At first, the "out of sight, out of mind" principle applied to objects and people in her life. If she could not see something, it may as well not exist. Now, however, peek-a-boo games with toys and dropping objects out of her direct line of sight take on new meaning. She will begin to visually search for the objects, which indicates her grasping the concept that things continue to exist even when she does not know where the objects are.

Therefore, play variations of peek-a-boo games by covering part of your face, covering parts of toys, dropping items in front of your baby, and hiding toys under and behind things like pillows and blankets.

❑

Using the banner you suspended beside her crib in the first month, point out and discuss the various shapes, colors, and patterns.

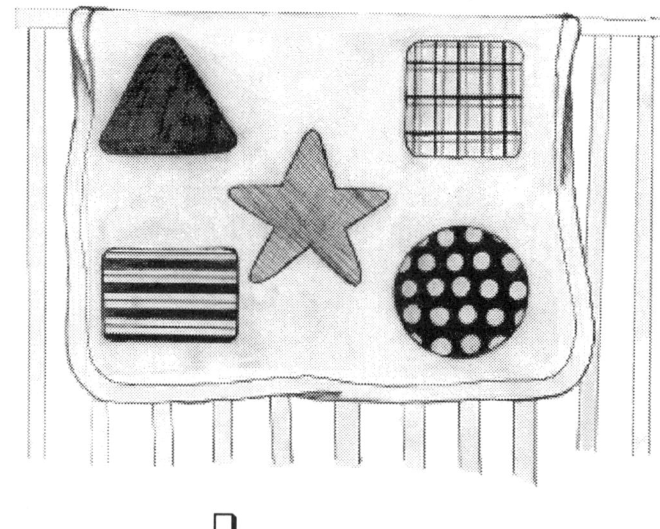

❑

To improve your baby's concept of space and time, hand her things differently. Rather than simply putting a toy in her hand, hold the toy in front of her and gradually move it toward her until she reaches for it. As with all of the recommended activities, repetition is important for learning in the first two or three years. Try varying the size of the toy you hand her to see how it affects when she begins to reach for it.

❑

To further encourage her reaching ability, hand things to your baby from different places around her so that she must reach up and to the left, then down and to the right, and so on.

❑

Introduce your baby to pull toys.

❑

Play piñata-type games with your baby to let her explore the effect of her actions on objects. Dangle a toy in front of her and give her a safe baton, such as a spoon or toothbrush, and allow her to strike the object. Mirror her amazement at the result.

❑

Hold your baby in front of a mirror and get him to notice the reflection of a toy in the mirror. Move the toy in and out of his view by moving it behind his and back out again.

❑

Make crawl-through tunnels from cardboard boxes. Attach various materials (sandpaper, silk, egg cartons, craft fur, etc.) to the interior walls for your child's discovery.

❑

Fill plastic bags with shaving cream or shampoo and put crayons, beads, and other small items inside. Seal the bags with tape and let your baby feel the different shapes.

❑

Fill a shoe box with cotton balls and hide ping pong balls, plastic blocks, wooden rings, or similar items inside. Show your baby how to fish for the items. Talk about each discovery.

Chapter 16 — Eight to Twelve Months

Your baby's memory can now keep track of his own actions, allowing him to initiate activities with the end result as a goal. He remembers that yesterday a plastic duck popped up when he pressed the red button on his pop-up toy. He wants to see the duck, so he presses the red button.

He can search for items manually, demonstrating that he now understands that things continue to exist though he does not see them. When you hide something behind your back, he will move around you to look for the item.

He can anticipate consequences and has begun to recognize the significance of space and time in the world around him. He also has a basic concept of quantity and is forming mental images of some events.

It is during this period that he begins speaking, taking turns, and imitating actions he has seen on a regular basis. He begins recognizing categories such as colors and shapes, as well. Therefore, his problem-solving skills are really beginning to take off. Your baby is now quite capable of setting goals and achieving them, an ability that will likely drive you to exhaustion before long! While you encourage his exercising this new skill, remember that your role as parent is

BUILDING SELF-ESTEEM THROUGH PLAY

Through much of your baby's first year, he is gradually beginning to recognize himself as separate from the world around him. He begins to understand the difference between his hands and his toys, between himself and you. This discovery is necessary, but you probably are just as concerned that he feel good about the self he is beginning to know. While he may be very smart and/or handsome, it may be more beneficial to praise other qualities.

When he works tirelessly at stacking blocks, you could say, "What a hard worker you are! I'm so proud of you." If he becomes frustrated at his inability to place rings on a cone, console him with, "That looks hard, but you really tried. Great job! I bet you could roll that ring across the floor if you wanted to." Play should be fun and your baby will do something each time that he can feel good about. Let him know you feel good about it too.

one of providing guidance as to which means of achieving goals are acceptable and which are not.

You will want to notice whether your baby tends to focus more on toys with the same color or if he seems to touch toys in a color sequence. If so, emphasize the color names as you play. If he seems more aware or interested in toy shapes, emphasize the shape names as you play. If he seems to play with everything randomly, just enjoy the fun.

ACTIVITIES

Music, reading, singing, language tapes, and talking are still very important parts of your baby's everyday life. He now has full visual range, meaning that he sees as far as he will ever see.

You can really begin challenging your baby with games that demonstrate cause and effect, requiring problem solving. (Examples of these types of games are included in this chapter's activities.) He will begin to imitate more and more of what you do and say. Therefore, you can teach your baby by merely performing demonstrations and allowing him to imitate your actions. Try incorporating one or more of the following activities into each day.

❑

Show your baby what happens when you wind a music box. He is accustomed to toys only making noise when they are shaken or squeezed. Let him see that there are other ways to reach a goal.

❑

Urge your baby to go after a ball that has rolled beyond his reach and bring it back to you. Your object is not to teach him to fetch but to teach him that he can change his situation: The ball is too far away; no problem. He only has to retrieve it.

❑

Present your baby with a container full of cotton balls and demonstrate how to use various utensils (a tablespoon, a plastic shovel, a wooden spoon, his fingers) to remove the cotton balls. Use the words "in" and "out" as you go.

❑

Line up three or four blocks on the floor and show your baby how pushing the first block makes all three of them move.

❑

Introduce your baby to percussion instruments like drums and xylophones, not so much for their musical influence as for their obvious cause and effect value.

❑

Hold a toy within your baby's reach, but do not release the toy when he tries to grab it. Let him know what means are acceptable for him reaching his goal of obtaining the toy.

❑

Play pat-a-cake and other rhyming games.

❑

Take turns making faces with your baby.

❑

Take turns imitating each other's sounds. However, when you repeat his sounds, change the number of syllables in the sound. For example, if your baby says "ba-ba", you say "ba-ba"; if he says it again, you say "ba-ba-ba." Keep using the three syllables until he imitates the three syllables. Be sure to stop if he gets irritated or begins losing interest in the game.

❑

Pat yourself on the head, and wait for your baby to imitate you. If he does not imitate you on his own, gently lift his hand to pat him on his head. Rub your stomach and wait for him to imitate you, and so on.

❑

Begin to introduce your baby to pretending by giving him a paper towel's cardboard roll. Press the numbers on a handheld telephone in front of him. Allow him time to pretend his cardboard roll is his telephone.

❑

Bowl a toy over with a ball in front of your baby to demonstrate how other objects can cause reactions.

❑

Demonstrate how to play with toy cars and trucks.

❑

Hide a music box or similar toy under a blanket while it is making its sounds. Let your baby search for and find the toy.

❑

Play hide-and-seek games with your baby's toys. Put a toy inside a pot in front of him and then cover the pot. Let him discover the toy inside when he opens the lid.

❑

With your baby watching, wrap a rattle or other noise-making toy in paper or paper towel. Hand the toy to him and help him unwrap it.

❑

Show your baby how nesting toys fit inside one another, and let him try to imitate the pattern.

❑

Show your baby how to place small (but too big to swallow) objects into a canister or shoe box and take them out again.

❑

Place a doll or some other favored toy on a blanket so that if your baby grabs too wildly at it, it falls out of his reach. This helps him learn to control his movements. Then place the same toy under a shoe box so that he cannot discern the shape of the toy or see evidence that it is there and encourage him to look for the toy.

❑

Show your baby how to slide a colorful piece of fabric through a paper towel's cardboard roll.

❑

Show your baby how sponges soak up water in the bath tub. Let him feel the weight of the dry sponge and then the weight of the wet sponge.

Chapter 17 — Twelve to Eighteen Months

Your toddler can now experiment through trial-and-error to find solutions to her problems and to accomplish her goals. She has a relative understanding of space, time, and the way things fit together. She is beginning to visualize objects rather than having to taste, touch, smell, hear, or see them to know they exist. She is also beginning to recognize the significance of words in representing people and things. Her imagination will soon take flight, and there are specific activities that reinforce her problem-solving skills, as well as those that prepare her to enter the world of make-believe.

ACTIVITIES

Music, reading, singing, language tapes, and talking are still very important parts of your toddler's everyday life. She may enjoy activities that you find unacceptable, such as throwing things or knocking things down. These activities can actually be used to stimulate her intellectual growth if you can kindly channel them into experiments that fascinate her. Provide her with lots of concrete learning materials (even simple household items) that she can pick up, roll, punch, stack, squeeze, bounce, pound, push, pull, and generally interact with. Now, try incorporating one or more of the following activities into each day.

MOTOR SKILL DEVELOPMENT: GAINING COORDINATION

During her first year of life, your baby worked hard learning to use her arms and legs, hands and feet, lips and tongue, eyes and ears, and just about everything in between. During her second year she will continue to work hard, fine-tuning her newly acquired skills. Up to this point, you probably did most of the stacking and she did most of the toppling. Now she will try her hand at stacking and at standing things upright. As she becomes more steady on her feet, she will love to carry toys around with her, waving them in the air just because she can. Congratulate her accomplishments as she masters the use of that complex machine, her own body.

Let your toddler experiment with different construction elements, whether they be a commercial set of building blocks or an assortment of household objects, such as shoeboxes, cardboard tubes, safe coffee cans, oatmeal boxes, plastic bowls, plastic cups, and so on.

❑

Make a game of placing a toy on the side of your baby's playpen so that she can knock it off the edge. Put the item back in a slightly different spot or at a different angle. She will be fascinated by the difference the change makes in how the toy falls or where it lands. Vary the size and weight of the toys you use in this experiment.

❑

Make a photo album of snapshots of people and toys that your toddler cherishes. Glue the pictures on both sides of a piece of cardboard or stiff paper. (You can print the names of the people and things beneath the pictures if you like.) Put each two-sided sheet in a plastic bag and seal the openings of the bags with sturdy tape. Punch holes in the taped edges and put metal rings through the holes. This may sound overly elaborate, but it will mean so much to your toddler.

❑

Use the same method above to make a food album. Instead of snapshots, cut out pictures of fruits, vegetables, breads, pastas, etc., and label them.

❑

Build simple inclines and hand your child a rolling toy (car, truck, tractor, ball, etc.) and stand other toys (tall wooden blocks or other easily toppled toys) at the bottom of the incline. Allow him to experiment with the whole setup as he sees fit.

❑

In a play area free of breakable objects, demonstrate how to twirl a ball inside a sock and allow your toddler to try it.

❑

Teach your toddler about the affect of resistance by allowing her to play with rolling toys on different surfaces, such as hard floors, carpeted or blanketed floors, grass, sand, gravel, etc.

❑

Similarly, demonstrate the effect of various surfaces on bouncing toys by dropping balls on the different floors and grounds described above.

❑

Place a collection of pictures of everyday objects (balls, cars, apples, cups, spoons and bowls, etc.) in front of your toddler. Next set the actual objects they represent in front of her and encourage her to match the picture to the object it represents.

❑

Show your toddler how to toss balls of socks, body puffs, etc., into a laundry basket or large box.

❑

Give your toddler a nearly empty tissue box and a completely empty tissue box. When she pulls a tissue out, teach her to roll the tissue into a ball and stuff it into the empty tissue box. Be sure to describe "in" and "out" as you go. Be as silly as your toddler would like. If she would rather put the tissue on your head just to watch it fall off, make that the game for now.

❑

Place a toy on the far end of a towel with the opposite end near your baby. This allows her to pull the towel towards her to retrieve the toy in addition to the option of going to the toy.

❑

Give your toddler a screw top jar and a number of small toys with which to fill and empty it.

❑

In a sandbox or safe play area, give your child a small pitcher or plastic measuring cup so that she can experiment with the effects of pouring water on heaps of sand or dirt.

❑

Show your toddler how to thread beads on a straw, but watch her closely to be sure she does not swallow the beads or insert them in her nose or ears.

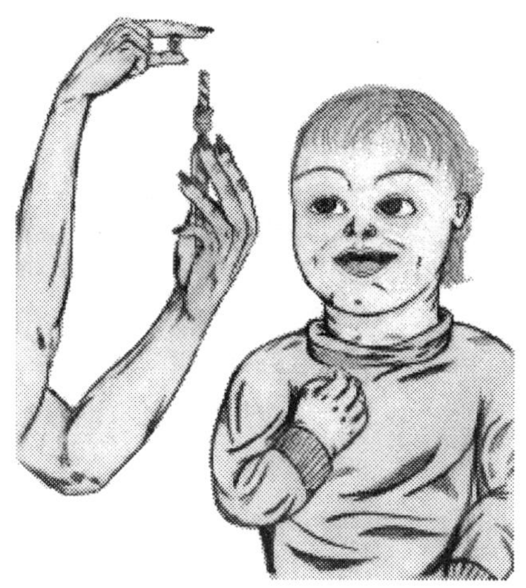

❑

Provide your toddler with multiples of the same item to play with at once, such as pillows, large buttons (watch her closely!), wooden or plastic blocks, etc.

❑

Now is a good time to let your toddler play with hammer boards, popping toys, and activity sets.

❑

Hand your toddler a toy sideways so that it does not fit through the slats of his crib unless he turns it.

❑

Continue to play rhyming games like pat-a-cake with your toddler and introduce similar games.

❑

Teach your toddler songs that require specific, coordinated body movements, such as, "This is the way we touch our nose, touch our nose, touch our nose," etc.

❑

Continue to encourage her to play with nesting and stacking toys.

❑

When your child is playing with percussion instruments, strike the instrument three times to see if your toddler can imitate you. Vary the rhythm and number of beats for her imitation.

❑

Either buy or make a shape sorter, preferably of varying colors and definitely of varying shapes, such as three-dimensional triangles, circles, squares, rectangles, and stars, naming each shape and color or pattern, such as stripes, dots, and solids.

❑

Present your toddler with pull toys or rolling toys that have coordinating peg people or animals.

❑

Allow her to push a doll carriage or miniature shopping cart.

❑

Allow your toddler to play with plastic blocks that interlock or pop in or out of each other.

❑

Present your toddler with puzzles having a few large pieces, perhaps even with knobs on each piece. Show her how the pieces fit together, but do not push her to perform.

❑

Fill a measuring cup with water and allow your toddler to try to pour the water into different size measuring cups, pointing out the difference in water level in each cup.

❑

Place clothespins in a large transparent container; then place small toys into large envelopes and let your toddler play with them.

❑

Introduce your toddler to a scooter, preferably one which requires her to put both feet on the floor or ground.

❑

Provide your child with large cardboard boxes of varying sizes for her exploration and imagination. Make sure the boxes are either indoors or are in a safe place without the possibility of someone striking the box not realizing your child is inside.

❑

Continue to make a game of wrapping and unwrapping toys in various materials that require folding, zipping, snapping, hooking, etc.

❑

Give your child plastic cups and containers in the bathtub and allow him to experiment with filling and emptying them with water.

❑

Stack blocks of the same color, but place a different color block in the middle of the stack. Let your child discover what happens if he removes the middle block.

❑

Make pull toys by attaching yarn to cardboard boxes and other non-pull toys.

❑

Cover one side of a cardboard tube with colored paper. Mirror your toddler's interest when he discovers that it changes color as he turns the tube.

❑

Demonstrate how large plastic nuts and bolts screw together, then allow him to play and experiment with them.

❑

Allow your toddler to help you with household duties, like dusting, folding laundry, cleaning dishes, and so on; or allow her to pretend to perform these duties in her own "house" consisting of a pup tent or blankets strewn across chairs.

❑

Have a great day at the beach without leaving home. Give your toddler an empty pan, a pan of dry oats or grits, and a spoon. Demonstrate how to shovel the "sand" from one pan to the other. Make experiments possible by providing funnels, cups, cookie cutters, and any other household items which could create interesting results.

Chapter 18 — Eighteen to Twenty-Four Months

Each passing stage of your baby's intellectual development is even more exciting than the last. Now, during this six-month period, your toddler becomes totally capable of independent thought. He can imagine, he can pretend, he can conceive of new ideas, and he can grasp symbolic mental pictures. How amazing! Prepare to marvel at the insight your little wonder will begin to show as he mentally constructs solutions to the challenges he faces. During this stage it is more important than ever to merely present your toddler with opportunities to learn, rather than directly trying to teach him. Make it possible for him to initiate his own educational activities by providing him with the supplies he needs, along with your own interested supervision.

ACTIVITIES

Music, reading, singing, language tapes, and talking are still very important parts of your toddler's everyday life. Continue to expand on the suggestions listed in previous chapters and incorporate at least one of the following suggestions each day.

❑

Continue to present your child with nesting toys, stacking toys, and shape sorters.

❑

Encourage your child's use of imagination with toy telephones, cash registers, and other toy replicas of objects from your world.

❑

Allow your toddler to imitate you in his own world as you complete tasks in your world. If you are painting, give him a spare brush and a bucket of water or of imaginary paint to use on a different area of the wall. If you are cooking, give him a spare spoon and pot of mud pies or of imaginary stew to stir.

❑

Place obstacles in the way of her push/pull toys and allow her to decide how to handle the situation.

❑

Provide your child with costumes and/or your old clothes in which to play dress up or just to pretend to act out other people in social situations.

❑

Encourage your child to dance to the music as you play it for him throughout the day.

❑

Provide your toddler with dolls or hand puppets and demonstrate how these can come to life: make them sneeze, pretend they are sleeping, pretend they are dancing, etc. Let your child take over from there.

❑

Introduce your child to finger paints.

❑

Provide your child with molding clay or dough. You can make your own by cooking one cup of flour, one-half cup of salt, two teaspoons of cream of tartar, and one tablespoon of oil together with food coloring. Let him use plastic knives and cookie cutters to discover the joys of this long-time favorite plaything.

❑

When pointing out and naming face and body parts, explain the purpose or use of each part.

❑

Provide your toddler with clean, empty milk jugs for him to fill with water, sand, gravel, cereal, or anything else he can think of.

❑

Allow your toddler to experiment with squeeze bottles and squirt toys in the bath tub.

❑

Provide your toddler with opportunities to strengthen fine motor skills by letting him peel a banana and with similar activities.

❑

If you pick up a yellow block, ask your baby to hand you another yellow block. Vary the game by asking for toys by size, color, and texture using only one feature at a time.

❑

Encourage your toddler's creative and artistic inclinations by providing him with scrap paper and crayons. Supervision is advisable if you do not want your walls to be considered artistic canvases.

❑

Play "horsie" and other rough and tumble games with your toddler in a safe area on a soft surface.

❑

Using age appropriate scissors and paste, help your child make a collage of pictures, yarn, rocks, and anything he finds interesting or attractive.

❑

Begin using simple explanations of time concepts: today, tomorrow, yesterday, this morning, tonight, etc.

❑

Help your child learn to string beads or dry pasta of different shapes and colors.

❑

Allow your toddler to indulge in experimental play with magnets: with each other and on the refrigerator.

❑

Allow your toddler to experiment with a magnifying glass.

❑

Play with your toddler with various types of balls and let him throw them through hula hoops, roll them over ramps and around obstacles, and so on.

❑

Decorate ping pong balls and put them in the cups of a muffin tin. Demonstrate the use of tongs in removing the balls.

❑

Give your toddler a container of clothespins and show him how to take them out one-by-one and attach them to the rim of the container, to each other, etc.

❑

Take your child to a playground or developmental play area with gyms or shapes to crawl through, around, and over.

❑

Provide your child with additional puzzles with large pieces; they no longer need have knobs attached to the pieces.

Chapter 19 — Warnings

Few people need to be told about the dangers of smoking. However, it must be stated that, if your goal is to enrich the environment of your child, you must not smoke in her presence. Studies show that secondary smoke has destructive effects on the minds and bodies of children.

Similarly, nursing mothers should also be aware of the negative affect that high caffeine consumption, as well as the consumption of alcohol and legal and illegal drugs, have on their babies. As long as you are nursing, view everything you take in as being fed to your baby.

Because children gather so much information from their environments, parents must also be conscious of the effect of television on their infants, babies, and toddlers. Television can be an important tool in teaching your child, but there are reasons for caution. First, television is quite a distraction, and, if it is not used discreetly, it may interfere with bonding. For instance, one mother noticed that while she nursed her baby in front of the television, her baby would turn to stare at the screen. Both mother and child were distracted from an opportunity to grow closer together. Secondly, could it also be possible that the constantly changing scenes on the screen contribute to some children's inability to concentrate or their tendency to bore easily? Do you want to try to keep pace with a cartoon character? Thirdly, studies have further shown that the content of many television programs have direct negative affects on the personalities of children.

The first two years of your child's life will go by much too fast. Enjoy every moment of it!

Appendix A — Enriched Development Checklist

Appendix A — Enriched Development Checklist

Use this information to evaluate your baby's home environment or child care center.[86]

Individual Attention

___ Baby will be held when he wants or needs to be held.

___ Baby will spend only a short amount of time in a swing, crib, bouncing chair, or playpen.

___ Baby will not stay in wet or dirty diapers for very long.

___ Baby will have someone to listen and respond when he talks.

___ Baby will be given eye contact when spoken to and will be spoken to with parentese in words he is learning to understand.

___ Baby will be read to frequently.

___ Baby will be massaged for at least 15 minutes every day.

___ Baby will be worn in a sling or pouch-like carrier several hours every day (birth to one year of age).

___ Baby will be made to feel special and appreciated for who he is and what he is.

Environment

___ Baby has a number of places to:

see himself	pull himself up	reach	kick
jump	climb up	climb over	climb on
climb in	go through	go under	go in and out

___ Baby has a number of different places to explore and play that have different light, texture, sound, smell, walls, and points of view.

___ Baby can go outside every day and can go for stroller or wagon rides every day.

___ Baby can get out of the stroller/wagon throughout the ride to explore on his own.

___ Baby can play with messy things like water, sand, dough, and paint.

___ Baby can reach a variety of toys and safe everyday objects.

___ Baby has a number of things to transport, push, pull, collect, dump, and throw.

___ Baby can listen to tuneful music and will be exposed to languages other than his native language.

___ Baby will receive proper nutrition and adequate sleep.

Appendix B — Your Child's Growth: Developmental Milestones

Appendix B — Your Child's Growth: Developmental Milestones

This information is used with permission of American Academy of Pediatrics, "Your Child's Growth; Developmental Milestones," brochure, Rev. 1999, American Academy of Pediatrics Copyright 1990, 1999. Milestones adapted with permission from William Frankenburg, M.D., and Josiah Dodds, M.D.

Guidelines for Parents

Watching a young child grow is a wonderful and unique experience for a parent. Learning to sit up, walk, and talk are some of the more major developmental "milestones" your child will achieve. But your child's growth is a complex and ongoing process. Young bodies are constantly going through a number of physical and mental changes.

Although no two children develop at the same rate, they should be able to do certain things at certain ages. As a parent, you are in the best position to note your child's development, and you can use the milestones described below as guidelines.

At the ages noted, observe your child for 1 month. (This lets you take into account any days when your child may be acting differently because he or she is sick or upset.) Use the milestones listed for each age to see how your child is developing.

Remember a "no" answer to any of these questions does not necessarily mean that there is a problem. Every child develops at his or her own pace and may sometimes develop more slowly in certain areas than other children the same age. Keep in mind these milestones should be used only as guidelines.

Plan to talk about these guidelines with your pediatrician during your next office visit if you note the following:

• major differences between your child's development and the "milestones"

• your child does not yet do many of the things usually done at his or her age

3 Months

When your baby is lying on his back, does he move each of his arms equally well? Check "no" if your child makes jerky or uncoordinated movements with one or both of his arms or legs, or uses only one arm all the time. Yes No

Does your child make sounds such as gurgling, cooing, babbling, or other noises besides crying? Yes No

Does your baby respond to your voice? Yes No

Are your child's hands frequently open? Yes No

When you hold your child in the upright position, can he support his head for more than a moment? Yes No

6 Months

Have you seen your baby play with her hands by touching them together? Yes No

Does your child turn his head to sounds that originate out of his immediate area? Yes No

Has your baby rolled over from her stomach to her back or from back to stomach? Yes No

When you hold your baby under his arms, can he bear some weight on his legs? Check "Yes" only if he tries to stand on his feet and supports some of his weight. Yes No

When your child is on his stomach, can he support his weight on outstretched hands? Yes No

Does your baby see small objects such as crumbs? Yes No

9 Months

When your child is playing and you come up quietly behind him, does he sometimes turn his head as though he hears you? (Loud sounds do not count.) Check "Yes " only if you have seen him respond to quiet sounds or whispers. Yes No

Can your child sit without support and without holding up her body with her hands? Yes No

Does your baby crawl or creep on her hands and knees? Yes No

Does your baby hold his bottle? Yes No

12 Months

When you hide behind something or around a corner and then reappear again, does your baby look for you or eagerly plan for you to reappear? Yes No

Does your baby make "ma-ma" or "da-da" sounds? Check "Yes" if she makes either sound. Yes No

Does your baby pull up to stand? Yes No

Does your baby say at least one word? Yes No

Does your baby walk holding on to furniture? Yes No

Is your baby able to locate sounds by turning her head? Yes No

18 Months

Can your child hold a regular cup or glass without help and drink from it without spilling? Yes No

Can your child walk all the way across a large room without falling or wobbling from side to side? Yes No

Does your child walk without support or help? Yes No

Does your child say at least two words? Yes No

Does your child take off his shoes by himself? Yes No

Does your child feed himself? Yes No

2 Years

Can your child say at least three specific words, other than "da-da" and "ma-ma," that mean the same thing each time they are said? Yes No

Can your child take off clothes such as pajamas (tops or bottoms) or pants? (Diapers, hats, and socks do not count.) Yes No

Does your child run without falling? Yes No

Does your child look at pictures in a picture book? Yes No

Does your child tell you what she wants? Yes No

Does your child repeat words others say? Yes No

Does your child point to at least one named body part? Yes No

As a parent, you are in the best position to note these subtle aspects of your child's behavior. These clues signal that your child's development is on schedule or that something might be wrong. A "no" answer to any of the questions may be a warning sign; make sure to bring it to your pediatrician's attention. Remember, these milestones are an aid, and not a test.

If you have any questions, plan to discuss them with your pediatrician. Pediatricians are trained to detect and treat developmental problems in children. Many problems, if detected early, can be treated by your pediatrician and successfully managed.

The information contained in this publication should not be used as a substitute for the medical care and advice of your pediatrician. There may be variations in treatment that your pediatrician may recommend based on individual facts and circumstances.

End of reprinted article.

Appendix C — Parental Depression and Child Development

Appendix C — Parental Depression and Child Development

Babies of depressed caregivers experience developmental delays without intervention. Because parents or other care givers who suffer from depression can have a negative impact, you should know what can be done. The following information has been prepared to help prevent, identify, and treat postpartum depression (PPD), although the information can benefit those with other forms of depression as well.

PREVENTING PPD

> The following article by Randi Hutter Epstein, M.D., originally appeared in the June 1999 issue of *Parents* magazine with the title "10 Ways to Prevent Postpartum Depression," Copyright ©1999 Gruner + Jahr Publishing. Reprinted from *Parents* magazine by permission.[87]

The last thing you want to think about during pregnancy is the possibility that after nine months of anticipation, you'll be too unhappy to enjoy your baby. Yet the truth is that 90 percent of new mothers have severe mood swings, known as baby blues, and 10 percent suffer major postpartum depression (PPD) in the first year.

Traditionally, doctors have blamed PPD on the dramatic drop in hormones that occurs after delivery. But chemistry can't explain everything; otherwise, all new mothers would plummet into depression. According to the latest research, women who suffer from PPD show clear warning signs during pregnancy; many have risk factors, such as a history of depression. "Doctors can detect the most vulnerable women early and prevent the illness before it strikes," says lead researcher Zachary Stowe, M.D., director of the Pregnancy and Postpartum Mood Disorders Program at Emory University, in Atlanta.

"The women with PPD in our study all had symptoms of anxiety or depression during pregnancy," says Dr. Stowe. However, doctors usually ignore these signs. "If a pregnant woman cries frequently, has trouble sleeping, and can't concentrate, everyone assumes that's typical," he adds.

In addition to talking to your doctor about any symptoms of distress that you're experiencing now, the best way to prevent PPD is to have realistic expectations. All new moms must adjust to having less control over their day-to-day lives, but some women find this overwhelming, which leads to anxiety and depression. Some ups and downs are inevitable, but the way you prepare for parenthood now can safeguard your well-being after the baby is born.

1 **Learn to chill out.** Many studies have shown that newborns bond better with calm mothers. New moms who spend at least 15 minutes every other day relaxing — whether by deep breathing, meditating or soaking in the tub — cope with the stresses of motherhood better than those who don't, according to Diane Sanford, Ph.D., author of *Postpartum Survival Guide* (New Harbinger Publications, 1994).

In the course for new mothers she teaches in St. Louis, Missouri, Dr. Sanford asks each student to report what she's done to create her "moments of self-preservation." Telling women to take it easy seems to relieve their guilt, Dr. Sanford says — perhaps because they see it as an assignment instead of an indulgence.

2 **Vow to sleep when your baby sleeps.** Everyone has heard the classic adage to nap when the baby naps, but too many women fail to actually heed the advice — using the downtime instead as a chance to make the bed or write thank-you notes. However, new mothers who are able to make up for lost sleep are less likely to feel depressed, according to a study by Michael O'Hara, Ph.D., of the University of Iowa, in Iowa City. "You may need friends, family members, or hired help to pitch in so you can get the sleep you deserve," says Dr. O'Hara, author of *Postpartum Depression: Causes and Consequences* (Sprinter-Verlag, 1994).

3 **Make time to exercise.** A recent study of more than 1,000 mothers found that those who exercised before and after the birth of their baby tended to feel better emotionally and were more social than women who didn't. "Taking a brisk walk, getting fresh air, and enjoying nature can improve your outlook," says Karen Rosenthal, Ph.D., a

psychologist in Westport, Connecticut. Don't push yourself to do strenuous aerobics, though; this is more about getting your blood flowing than burning calories or tightening your abdominal muscles.

4 **Think of motherhood as a career change.** "I often tell couples that parenthood is a job, but it's not 9 to 5; it's 24 hours a day," says Dr. Rosenthal. Most women expect that the first few months of a new job will be stressful, but they often don't anticipate the tensions involved with mothering a newborn. Denise Madison, a New York City mother of twins, said she became much happier once she started telling herself, "My babies are my job" — and that everything else, including reading the newspaper could wait.

5 **Don't expect to be the perfect parent.** Rest assured, every mom can tell you stories about having left the house with her shirt inside out or having forgotten to put a diaper on her baby after a middle-of-the-night changing. Many women with PPD are perfectionists, notes Joyce A. Venis, a psyciatric nurse and president of Depression After Delivery Inc., a self-help group based in Raritan, New Jersey. "They feel guilty if they can't do everything right and presume that every other mother is doing a better job," she says. "As a result, they impose unrealistic expectations upon themselves." Your goal is not to fulfill some notion of the ideal mother but to be a happy parent.

6 **Plan to get plenty of help.** You'll have to delegate chores, let friends bring dinner over, and invite your sister or mother to watch the baby so you can go shopping. "If you feel overwhelmed or resentful, you need to give yourself permission to ask for help rather than wait for others to offer," says Dr. Stanford.

7 **Confront your fears.** Have a conversation with your husband in which you each list three things that frighten you about parenthood, suggests Jane Israel Honikman, founder of Postpartum Support International, in Santa Barbara, California. They can be emotional concerns — such as that the two of you won't have enough time alone — or practical anxieties about colic or breast-feeding.

8 **Be flexible.** You need to be able to go with the flow. "Your morning shower and coffee may not happen until noon," says Dr. Rosenthal. What's more, you should realize that there will be days when taking a shower is the only thing you can check off your

to-do list. Rather than panic about how chaotic your life is, try to appreciate its unpredictability — and throw away that list!

9 **Join or start a new-mothers group.** "Isolation breeds anxiety," says Sally Placksin, author of *Mothering the New Mother* (Newmarket Press, 1993). Just knowing that others are experiencing the same mix of joy and frustration will put your mind at ease. "It's also helpful to find a calm, experienced friend who can not only show you how to bathe and burp the baby but who will understand how you're feeling," says Placksin. "You need adult contact," agrees Denise Madison. "When my twins were 4 weeks old, I started feeling sorry for myself. It just became easier to stay home than to get out of the house." One night, despite her reluctance, a neighbor insisted that Madison come to a Christmas party with some neighborhood moms. Listening to others talk — and having adult conversation — pulled her out of the doldrums.

ARE YOU AT RISK?

The key to minimizing postpartum depression (PPD) is spotting symptoms months before the baby is born, say Zachary Stowe, M.D., an assistant professor of psychiatry and obstetrics and gynecology, and director of the Pregnancy and Postpartum Mood Disorders Program at Emory University, in Atlanta.

Symptoms of depression include insomnia, lack of concentration, fearfulness, lack of appetite, anxiety for no apparent reason, irritability, an overwhelming sense of failure, and hopelessness. If you have several of these symptoms, talk to your obstetrician immediately to discuss your options.

Depression during pregnancy, as at any other time, can be treated with therapy and/or medication. Increasing evidence shows that certain medications, including Prozac, have no adverse effect (even in the first trimester) on an unborn or nursing baby.

10 **Remind yourself that the best is yet to come.** Between hormonal swings and all the changes in your life, it will be a challenge to feel confident sometimes — especially if you assume this is supposed to be the best time of your life. Focus on the light at the end of the tunnel: Soon your baby will settle into a schedule, breastfeeding will be second nature, and your diaper bag will be stocked so you can get out of the house quickly. You have years of best times ahead; don't convince yourself that they need to be the first weeks or months of motherhood.

End of reprinted article.

RECOGNIZING PPD

Experts at the University of Edinburgh have developed a scale that helps healthcare professionals more easily identify postpartum depression. A healthcare professional using this scale would ask you to rate the severity of your symptoms, such as your ability to laugh at and look forward to things, whether you blame yourself unnecessarily for things, whether you feel extraordinarily anxious or panicky, whether you are having trouble sleeping or trouble coping with things in general, about how much you have been crying, and whether you have considered harming yourself. If your baby is two weeks old and you still have concerns about any of these issues, seek the advice of a qualified health care provider.

IMPACT OF CAREGIVER'S DEPRESSION

Babies in the care of parents or others suffering depression experience a number of adverse effects emotionally, intellectually, and physically. Such babies:

- are less responsive,

- have sleep problems,

- have elevated levels of stress hormones (which damages brain connections),

- show activity in the part of the brain that handles negative emotions (the negative behavior increases also, such as avoiding eye contact and displaying sad or angry expressions),

- show signs of neurologic delays,

- use less social referencing (looking to caregivers for information),

- display fewer interested expressions,

- play less,

- explore less,

- experience delayed growth,

- have more difficulty matching happy facial expressions with happy vocal expressions, and

- have lower IQ scores.

At the time these babies reach preschool age, they continue to have problems interacting with others and coping with stress.

EFFECTIVE INTERVENTIONS FOR BABY

Interaction with a non-depressed father or other caregiver can act as a natural buffer and can compensate for the negative effects of maternal depression on babies. Also, according to researcher Tiffany Field, Ph.D., of the Touch Research Institute, massage therapy was more effective than rocking in contributing "to more organized sleep patterns, more positive interaction behaviors, and greater weight gain."[88] Those infants who were massaged for 15 minutes per day, two days per week, were more responsive, cried less, had lower cortisol (stress hormone) levels, and better serotonin (the horomone that promotes a sense of well-being) levels. Of course, the best thing for the baby overall is for mom to feel better soon.

EFFECTIVE TREATMENTS FOR MOM

Dr. Field's research revealed that mothers suffering with PPD had significant short-term relief after listening to their favorite music for only 20 minutes and that massage therapy was equally beneficial. Furthermore, as noted in Dr. Epstein's above article on preventing PPD, anti-depressant drugs have been found to successfully treat depressed mothers with "no adverse effect (even in the first trimester) on an unborn or nursing baby."[89] Dr. Lisa Keller, an expert for *BabyTalk* online, echoes this conclusion by stating that a recent study published in the *Journal of the American Medical Association (JAMA)* "found no increase in miscarriages, malformations, stillbirth, or premature births among the women using SSRIs [selective seratonin reuptake inhibitors, such as Prozac] — a finding that concurs with most of the previous studies." Dr. Keller also states that a study reported on in the January 1997 *New England Journal of Medicine* "found that there was no difference in temperament, mood, behavior problems, language develpment or IQ levels" in children whose mothers took SSRI or tricyclic drugs during pregnancy.[90]

References

References

1.a. S. H. Jacob, Ph.D., 1991, *Your Baby's Mind* (Holbrook, Massachusetts: Bob Adams, Inc.), pp. 41-45.

b. Sharon Begley with Mary Hager, February 19, 1996, "Your Child's Brain," *Newsweek*, pp.56-62.

c. Lewis P. Lipsitt, Ph.D., November 5, 1998, "Learning and Emotion in Infants," *Pediatrics* Vol. 102 (5), pp. 1262-1267.

d. William Staso, Ph.D., December 1997, "'Windows of Opportunity' for Infants and Toddlers," [Internet, WWW], Available: Great Beginnings Press, Address: http://www.utech.net/gbpress/book1005/windowsop.htm.

e. William Staso, Ph.D., "What Stimulation Your Baby Needs to Become Smart," [Internet, WWW], Available: Great Beginnings Press, Address: http://www.utech.net/gbpress/book1005/smartinfo.htm.

f. "ABC 'Prime Time Live' Explores Your Child's Brain," 1995, *The Sound Beginnings Newsletter* Vol. 1 (1) [Internet, WWW], Available: Sound Beginnings, Address: http://www.soundbeginnings.com.

g. Mike, John, M.D. 1999. "Baby Brain Power Expanding the Mind Prenatally." *Childbirth Instructor Magazine.* [Internet, WWW]. Available: Brilliant Babies Powerful Adults, John Mike, M.D., Address: http://www.smart-baby.com/article-1 .htm.

h. Jenny Friedman, Ph.D., January 1998, "Genius?," *American Baby* Vol. LX (1), pp. 59-60.

i. Ronnie Polaneczky, March 1, 1998, "How Kids Get Smart: The Surprising News," *Redbook* Vol. 190, pp. 102-106,[Internet, WWW], Available: Electronic Library Fee-Based Service; Address: http://www.electroniclibrary.com. A copy of this article is available from the author.

j. Barbara Kantrowitz, Special Edition Spring/Summer 1997, "Off to a Good Start," *Newsweek*, pp. 6-9.

k. Sharon Begley with Andrew Murr, Special Edition Spring/Summer 1997, "How to Build a Baby's Brain," *Newsweek*, pp. 28-32.

l. "Train Your Child in the Right Way — And Do It from Infancy!," May 22, 1987, *Awake!*, pp. 7-11.

2. Jacob, p. 26.

3.a. Lansdown and Walker, p. 125.

b. Wingert and Underwood, pp. 12-15.

4.a. William Sears, M.D., and Martha Sears, R.N., undated, "Early Walkers, Late Walkers," *ParentTime* [Internet, WWW], Available: *Parenting's BabyTalk* website, Address: http://www.pathfinder.com/ParentTime/sears/leafs/earlywk.html.

b. Richard Lansdown and Marjorie Walker, 1991, *Your Child's Development from Birth through Adolescence* (New York, NY: Alfred A. Knopf, Inc.), p. 117.

c. Anne Underwood and Peter Plagens, Special Edition Spring/Summer 1997, "Little Artists and Athletes," *Newsweek*, pp. 14-15.

d. Pat Wingert and Anne Underwood, Special Edition Spring/Summer 1997, "Hey — Look Out, World, Here I Come," *Newsweek*, pp. 12-15.

5. "Your Child's Growth: Developmental Milestones," 1999, [Internet, WWW], Available: American Academy of Pediatrics; Address: http://www.aap.org/family/devmile.htm.

6. *Merriam-Webster's Collegiate Dictionary*, 10th ed., *s.v.* "intelligence."

7.a. *Parents*' Child Development Toys, *Balls in a Bowl Play & Learning Guide*, "Intelligence: All Kinds of Smart," N9562A 8363(USA:CNI), pp. 2-3. Published brochure. Available from the author.

b. Lansdown and Walker, p. 15-18.

8.a. "Learning Begins in the Womb," January 22, 1992, *Awake!*, p. 15.

b. Susan Ochshorn, undated, "How Smart Is Your Baby?," *Parenting* [Internet, WWW], Available: *Parenting's BabyTalk* website, Address: http://www.pathfinder.com/ParentTime/Growing/smartba.html?az.

9.a. Ronnie Polaneczky, March 1, 1998, "How Kids Get Smart: The Surprising News," *Redbook* Vol. 190, pp. 102-106,[Internet, WWW], Available: Electronic Library Fee-Based Service; Address: http://www.electroniclibrary.com. A copy of this article is available from the author.

b. William Greenough, Ph.D., Harry Chugani, M.D., and Craig Ramey, Ph.D., October 4, 1994. Interview by Michelle Trudeau, "Enriched Environments Positively Affect Intelligence," *All Things Considered*, National Public Radio. [Internet, WWW], Available: Electronic Library Fee-Based Service; Address: http://www.electroniclibrary.com. A copy of this article is available from the author.

c. Wingert and Underwood, p. 14.

10. Jacob, p. 42.

11.a. Jacob, pp. 41-45.

b. Begley, *et al*, *Newsweek* February 19, 1996, p.56-62.

c. Lipsitt, *Pediatrics* Vol. 102 (5), pp. 1262-1267.

d. Staso, "Windows of Opportunity."

e. Staso, "Become Smart."

f. "ABC 'Prime Time Live' Explores Your Child's Brain," 1995.

g. John Mike, M.D., "Baby Brain Power."

h. Friedman, pp. 59-60.

i. Polaneczky, pp. 102-106.

j. Kantrowitz, pp. 6-9.

k. Begley with Murr, pp. 28-32.

l. "Train Your Child," pp. 7-11.

12. Sidney Ledson, 1987, *Raising Brighter Children: A Program for Busy Parents* (New York, NY: Walker and Company), pp. 42-43.

13.a. Begley, *et al*, *Newsweek* February 19, 1996, p.56.

b. Mike, John, M.D. "Baby Brain Power."

14. Sharon Begley and Pat Wingert, April 28, 1997, "Teach Your Parents Well," *Newsweek*, p. 72.

15. Candace Erickson, M.D., "Emotional and Intellectual Development," in Nicholas Cunningham, M.D., Dr. P.H., Donald F. Tapley, M.D., Genell J. Subak-Sharpe, M.S., and Diane M. Goetz (eds.), 1990, *The Columbia University College of Physicians and Surgeons Complete Guide to Early Childcare* (New York, NY: Crown Publishers, Inc.), p. 147.

16. Jacob, p. 64-65.

17. "The Formative Years — What You Sow Now You Will Reap Later," September 22, 1992, *Awake!*, p. 6.

18.a. Jacob L. Gewirtz, Ph.D., and Albert R. Hollenbeck, Ph.D., "Effects on Parents of Contact/Touch in the Postpartum Hour," in Nina Gunzenhauser (ed.), 1990, *Advances in Touch: New Implications in Human Development*, Pediatric Round Table Series: 14 (USA: Johnson & Johnson Consumer Products, Inc.), pp. 70-71.

b. Jerry Adler, Special Edition Spring/Summer 1997, "It's a Wise Father Who Knows . . .," *Newsweek*, p. 73.

19.a. "The Formative Years — What You Sow Now You Will Reap Later," September 22, 1992, *Awake!*, p. 6.

b. "Train Your Child," pp. 7-11.

20. "Babies and Toddlers at Greater Risk in Child Care," October 21, 1997, [Internet, WWW], Available: Zero to Three; Address: http://www.zerotothree.org/baberisk.html.

21.a. "Family Communication — How Can It Be Improved?," January 8, 1985, *Awake!*, p. 6.

b. Anne Merriman, February 1998, "A Touching Development," *Parenting's BabyTalk* Vol. 63 (1), p. 29.

22. Geraldine Dawson, David Hessl, and Karin Frey, 1994, "Social Influences on Early Developing Biological and Behavioral Systems Related to Risk for Affective Disorder," *Development and Psychopathology* Vol. 6, pp. 759-779, summarized in "The Effect of Maternal Depression on Infant/Toddler Emotional Development," 1997, *Supplement to Module III Materials, The Program for Infant/Toddler Caregivers*. Unpublished Manuscript. [Internet, WWW], Available: Early Head Start National Resource Center; Address: http://www.ehsnrc.org/rmdepre.htm.

23.a. J. Madeleine Nash, February 3, 1997, "Special Report: Fertile Minds," *Time* Vol. 149 (5), p. 55.

b. Abstract in PubMed database: G. Dawson, K. Frey, H. Panagiotides, J. Osterling, and D. Hessl, February 1997, "Infants of Depressed Mothers Exhibit Atypical Frontal Brain Activity: A Replication and Extension of Previous Findings," *Journal of Child Psychology and Psychiatry* Vol. 38 (2), pp. 179-186, [Internet, WWW], Available: PubMed Database; Address: http://www.ncbi.nlm.nih.gov.

c. Abstract in PubMed database: G. Dawson, H. Panagiotides, L. G. Klinger, and S. Spieker, July 1997, "Infants of Depressed and Nondepressed Mothers Exhibit Differences in Frontal Brain Electrical Activity during the Expression of Negative Emotions," *Developmental Psychology* Vol. 33 (4), pp. 650-656, [Internet, WWW], Available: PubMed Database; Address: http://www.ncbi.nlm.nih.gov.

24.a. Polaneczky, pp. 102-106.

b. Begley with Murr, p. 32.

c. Merriman, p. 29.

25.a. Armin Brott, June/July 1997, "What a Difference a Dad Makes," *Parenting's BabyTalk* Vol. 62 (5), pp. 34-36.

b. "Research on Fatherhood — Old Discoveries Seem New Again," undated, [Internet, WWW], Available: Men's Health Network, Address: http://menshealthnetwork.org/library/mhndocs/Fatherhd.html.

c. Adler, p. 73.

d. David Popenoe, March 1, 1996, "A World without Fathers (Consequences of Children Living without Fathers)," *The Wilson Quarterly* Vol. 20, pp. 12-18, [Internet, WWW], Available: Electronic Library Fee-Based Service; Address: http://www.electroniclibrary.com. A copy of this article is available from the author.

e. Abstract in PubMed database: M. W. Yogman, D. Kindlon, and F. Earls, June 1996, "Father Involvement and Cognitive/Behavioral Outcomes of Preterm Infants," *Journal of the American Academy of Child and Adolescent Psychiatry* Vol. 35 (6), pp. 699-700, [Internet, WWW], Available: PubMed Database; Address: http://www.ncbi.nlm.nih.gov.

26. Brott, "Difference a Dad Makes," pp. 34-36.

27. "People — Why They Act the Way They Do," April 8, 1980, *Awake!*, p. 10.

28. "From the Cradle to the Grave, Our Greatest Need Is Love," September 22, 1986, *Awake!*, p. 4.

29. Martin Reite, M.D., "Effects of Touch on the Immune System," in Nina Gunzenhauser (ed.), 1990, *Advances in Touch: New Implications in Human Development*, Pediatric Round Table Series: 14 (USA: Johnson & Johnson Consumer Products, Inc.), pp. 22-31.

30. Michael Gullen, Ph.D. and Joan Lunden, April 4, 1997. "Parenting: The First Years Last Forever," *Good Morning America*, American Broadcasting Companies, Inc. [Internet, WWW], Available: Electronic Library Fee-Based Service; Address: http://

www.electroniclibrary.com. A copy of this transcript is available from the author.

31.a. Jacob, pp. 247-250.

b. William Sears, M.D., April 1999, "Smart from the Start," *Parenting's BabyTalk* Vol. 64 (3), p. 26.

c. William Sears, M.D., *The Baby Book*, special excerpt reprinted by NoJo, Inc., 1992, "BabyWearing: An Introduction to The Original Babysling," p. 2.

d. John H. Kennell, M.D., "Doula-Mother and Parent-Infant Contact," in Nina Gunzenhauser (ed.), 1990, *Advances in Touch: New Implications in Human Development*, Pediatric Round Table Series: 14 (USA: Johnson & Johnson Consumer Products, Inc.), p. 59.

e. Nicholas Cunningham, M.D., Dr. P.H., "Caring for the Newborn," in Nicholas Cunningham, M.D., Dr. P.H., Donald F. Tapley, M.D., Genell J. Subak-Sharpe, M.S., and Diane M. Goetz (eds.), 1990, *The Columbia University College of Physicians and Surgeons Complete Guide to Early Childcare* (New York, NY: Crown Publishers, Inc.), p. 19.

32.a. Linda Weber, September 1997, "Ready to Wear," *Parenting's BabyTalk* Vol. 62 (7), p. 50.

b. Bell, Allison. March 1999. "Let the Games Begin." *American Baby* Vol. LXI (3), pp. 38-43.

33. Ronald G. Barr, M.A., M.D.C.M., F.R.C..P.(C.), "Reduction of Infant Crying by Parent Carrying," in Nina Gunzenhauser (ed.), 1990, *Advances in Touch: New Implications in Human Development*, Pediatric Round Table Series: 14 (USA: Johnson & Johnson Consumer Products, Inc.), pp. 105-113.

34.a. Weber, pp. 50-51.

b. Cunningham (Nicholas), p. 19.

c. Ledson, p. 48.

35.a. Cassie Landers, Ed.D., M.P.H., "Child-Rearing Practices and Infant Development in South India," in Nina Gunzenhauser (ed.), 1990, *Advances in Touch: New Implications in Human Development*, Pediatric Round Table Series: 14 (USA: Johnson & Johnson Consumer Products, Inc.), p. 51.

b. Weber, p. 53.

36. Weber, p. 54.

37. Landers, p. 51.

38.a. Saul M. Schanberg, M.D., Cynthia M. Kuhn, Ph.D., Tiffany M. Field, Ph.D., and Jorge V. Bartolome, Ph.D., "Maternal Deprivation and Growth Suppression," in Nina Gunzenhauser (ed.), 1990, *Advances in Touch: New Implications in Human Development*, Pediatric Round Table Series: 14 (USA: Johnson & Johnson Consumer Products, Inc.), pp. 3-10.

b. Tiffany M. Field, Ph.D., and Saul M. Schanberg, M.D., "Massage Alters Growth and Catecholamine Production in Preterm Newborns," in Nina Gunzenhauser (ed.), 1990, *Advances in Touch: New Implications in Human Development*, Pediatric Round Table Series: 14 (USA: Johnson & Johnson Consumer Products, Inc.), pp. 101-103.

c. Sarah Van Boven, Special Edition Spring/Summer 1997, "Giving Infants a Helping Hand," *Newsweek*, p. 45.

39. Michael J. Meaney, Ph.D., David H. Aitken, M.Sc., Seema Bhatnagar, M.Sc., Shari R. Bodnoff, M.A., John B. Mitchell, Ph.D., and Alain Sarrieau, Ph.D., "Neonatal Handling and the Development of the Adrenocortical Response to Stress," in Nina Gunzenhauser (ed.), 1990, *Advances in Touch: New Implications in Human Development*, Pediatric Round Table Series: 14 (USA: Johnson & Johnson Consumer Products, Inc.), pp. 11-22.

40. Committee on Sports Medicine, 1986-1988, November 1988, "Infant Exercise Programs (RE8132)," *Pediatrics* Vol. 82 (5), p. 800, [Internet, WWW], Available: American Academy of Pediatrics; Address: http://www.aap.org/policy/02223.html.

41. Committee on Sports Medicine, 1984-1985, April 1985 (reaffirmed February 1990), "Infant Swimming Programs (RE5045)," *Pediatrics* Vol. 75 (4), [Internet, WWW], Available: American Academy of Pediatrics; Address: http://www.aap.org/policy/362.html.

42. *Merriam-Webster's Collegiate Dictionary*, 10th ed., s.v. "spoil."

43.a. L. John Horwood and David M. Fergusson, January 1998, "Breastfeeding and Later Cognitive and Academic Outcomes," *Pediatrics* Vol. 101 (1), [Internet, WWW], Available: American Academy of Pediatrics; Address: http://www.pediatrics.org/cgi/content/full/101/1/e9.

b. William Sears, M.D., April 1999, "Smart from the Start," *Parenting's BabyTalk* Vol. 64 (3), p. 24.

c. Daniel Glick, Special Edition Spring/Summer 1997, "Rooting for Intelligence," *Newsweek*, p. 32.

d. Dia L. Michels, April 1998, "Breastfeeding Is Best Feeding," *Parenting's BabyTalk*, Vol. 63 (3), p. 21.

44. "Mom, I Cannot Do Without You," August 22, 1977, *Awake!*, p. 8.

45.a. William Sears, M.D., April 1999, "Smart from the Start," *Parenting's BabyTalk* Vol. 64 (3), p. 24.

b. Elizabeth Ward, M.S., R.D., April 1999, "Smart Foods," *American Baby* Vol. LXI (4), p. 12.

46.a. Work Group on Breastfeeding, 1996 to 1997, December 1997, "Breastfeeding and the Use of Human Milk (RE9729)," *Pediatrics* Vol. 100 (6), pp. 1035-1039, [Internet, WWW], Available: American Academy of Pediatrics; Address: http://www.aap.org/policy/re9729.html.

b. "101 Reasons to Breastfeed Your Child," 1998, [Internet, WWW], Available: ProMoM, Inc.; Address: http://www.promom.org/101.

c. Allan S. Cunningham, M.D., "Nutrition in the First Year," in Nicholas Cunningham, M.D., Dr. P.H., Donald F. Tapley, M.D., Genell J. Subak-Sharpe, M.S., and Diane M. Goetz (eds.), 1990, *The Columbia University College of Physicians and Surgeons Complete Guide to Early Childcare* (New York, NY: Crown Publishers, Inc.), pp. 34-35.

d. "Breast-Feeding Basics," August 22, 1994, *Awake!*, pp. 10-13.

e. "Breast Feeding — A Mother's Loving 'Sacrifice'," June 8, 1983, *Awake!*, pp. 20-22.

f. "Why Breast-feeding Is Best Feeding," July 22, 1981, *Awake!*, pp. 21-23.

g. "Breastfeeding: The Best Start for Your Baby," December 1997, LF808 (Evansville, IN: Mead Johnson & Company), p. 2. Published brochure. Available from the author.

h. Michels, p. 21.

i. Bryan S. Vartabedian, M.D., April 1999, "Feed Me, Mommy," *American Baby* Vol. LXI (4), p. 62-67.

47.a. "Pacifiers Linked to a Decrease in Breastfeeding," March 1, 1999, Press Release, [Internet,WWW], Available: American Academy of Pediatrics; Address: http://www.pediatrics.org.

b. Cynthia R. Howard, Fred M. Howard, Bruce Lanphear, Elisabeth A. DeBlieck, Shirley Eberly, and Ruth A. Lawrence, March 1999, "The Effects of Early Pacifier Use on Breastfeeding Duration," *Pediatrics* Vol. 103 (3) p. e33, [Internet, WWW], Available: American Academy of Pediatrics; Address: http://www.pediatrics.org/cgi/content/full/103/3/e33.

c. Abstract in *Pediatrics* database: Cesar Gomes Victora, Dominique Pareja Behague, Fernando Celso Barros, Maria Teresa Anselmo Olinto, and Elizabeth Weiderpass, March 1997, "Pacifier Use and Short Breastfeeding Duration: Cause, Consequence, or Coincidence?," *Pediatrics* Vol. 99 (3), pp. 445-453, [Internet, WWW], Available: American Academy of Pediatrics; Address: http://www.pediatrics.org.

d. Abstract in *Pediatrics* database: F. C. Barros, C. G. Victora, T. C. Semer, S. Tonioli Filho, E. Tomasi, and E. Weiderpass, April 1995, "Use of Pacifiers Is Associated with Decreased Breast-feeding Duration," *Pediatrics* Vol. 95 (4), pp. 497-499, [Internet, WWW], Available: American Academy of Pediatrics; Address: http://www.pediatrics.org.

48.a. Abstract in *Pediatrics* database: M. Niemela, M. Uhari, and M. Mottonen, November 1995, "A Pacifier Increases the Risk of Recurrent Acute Otitis Media in Children in Day Care Centers," *Pediatrics* Vol. 96 (5), pp. 884-888, [Internet, WWW], Available: American Academy of Pediatrics; Address: http://www.pediatrics.org.

b. Abstract in *Pediatrics* database: Kate North, Peter Fleming, Jean Golding, and the ALSPAC Study Team, March 1999, "Pacifier Use and Morbidity in the First Six Months of Life," *Pediatrics* Vol. 103 (3), pp. E34, [Internet, WWW], Available: American Academy of Pediatrics; Address: http://www.pediatrics.org.

49. Committee on Nutrition, 1991 to 1992, Part 1 June 1992, "The Use of Whole Cow's Milk in Infancy (RE9251)," *Pediatrics* Vol. 89 (6), pp.1105-1109, [Internet, WWW], Available: American Academy of Pediatrics; Address: http://www.aap.org/policy/04788.html.

50. Richard Lansdown and Marjorie Walker, 1991, *Your Child's Development from Birth through Adolescence* (New York, NY: Alfred A. Knopf, Inc.), p. 83.

51.a. World Health Organization, "The International Code of Marketing of Breastmilk Substitutes," The International Baby Food Action Network, [Internet, WWW], Address: http://www.gn.apc.org/ibfan/fullcode.html.

b. Professor G. J. Ebrahim and Dr. William Cutting, 4th Quarter 1998, "Update on Breastfeeding," *Child Health Dialogue* Issue 9 [Internet, WWW], Available: World Health Organization; Address: http://www.who.int/chd/pub/newslet/dialog/9/update_on_breastfeeding.htm.

c. "Breast-Feeding Basics," August 22, 1994, *Awake!*, p. 13.

52.a. Work Group on Breastfeeding, 1996 to 1997, December 1997, "Breastfeeding and the Use of Human Milk (RE9729)," *Pediatrics*

Vol. 100 (6), pp. 1035-1039, [Internet, WWW]. Available: American Academy of Pediatrics; Address: http://www.aap.org/policy/re9729.html.

b. "Media Alert: AAP Reaffirms Breastfeeding Stance Following Fictional TV Show," 1999, American Academy of Pediatrics, [Internet, WWW], Available: American Academy of Pediatrics; Address: http://www.aap.org/visit/brmdalt.htm.

c. "101 Reasons to Breastfeed Your Child," 1998 [Internet, WWW], Available: ProMoM, Inc.; Address: http://www.promom.org/101.

d. "Breastfeeding: The Best Start for Your Baby," p. 2.

e. Michels, p. 21.

53. J. Larry Brown, Ph.D., and Lori P. Marcotte, M.S., M.P.H., R.D., January/February 1999, "Nutrition and Cognitive Development in Children," *Early Childhood News*, [Internet, WWW], Available: *Early Childhood News*; Address: http://www.earlychildhoodnews.com/archive/nutri.htm.

54. Vicki Lansky, 1979, *Feed Me! I'm Yours*, (New York, NY: Bantam Books).

55.a. Judith E. Foulke, September 1994, "Mercury in Fish: Cause for Concern?," *FDA Consumer* [Internet, WWW], Available: U.S. Food and Drug Administration, Address: http://vm.cfsan.fda.gov/~dms.

b. Sue Gilbert, M.S., 1999, "Fish Safety Concerns," ParentsPlace.com [Internet, WWW], Available: ParentsPlace.com, Address: http://www.parentsplace.com/expert/nutritionist/safety/qa/0,3488,12042,00.html.

56.a. William G. Crook, M.D., 1986, *The Yeast Connection* (New York, New York: Random House), pp. 189-204, 290-291, 377.

b. "Collected Net Articles of Dr. Kalle Reichelt," [Internet, WWW], Address: http://www.panix.com/~donwiss/reichelt.html.

c. Abstract in PubMed database: J. Breakey, June 1997, "Review: The Role of Diet and Behaviour in Childhood," *Journal of Paediatric Child Health* Vol. 33 (3), pp. 190-194 [Internet, WWW], Available: The Fiengold Association of the United States; Address: http://feingold.org/research.shtml.

d. Richard E. Layton, M.D., 1998, "Patient of the Month: Marshall," [Internet, WWW], Available: Allergy Connection, Address: http://www.allergyconnection.com/PATIENT/marshall.html.

e. Abstract in PubMed database: M. Boris and F. Mandel, May 1994, "Foods and Additives Are Common Causes of the Attention Deficit Hyperactive Disorder in Children," *Annals of Allergy* Vol. 72, pp. 462-468 [Internet, WWW], Available: The Fiengold Association of the United States; Address: http://feingold.org/research.shtml.

f. Abstract in PubMed database: T. M. Nsouli, S. M. Nsouli, R. E. Linde, F. O'Mara, R. T. Scanlon, and J. A. Bellanti, September 1994, "Role of Food Allergy in Serious Otitis Media," *Annals of Allergy* Vol. 73 (3), pp. 215-219 [Internet, WWW], Available: The Fiengold Association of the United States; Address: http://feingold.org/research.shtml.

g. Abstract in PubMed database: S. Schoenthaler, J. Moody, and L. Pankow, November 1, 1991, "Applied Nutrition and Behavior," *Journal of Applied Nutrition* Vol. 43[Internet, WWW], Available: The Fiengold Association of the United States; Address: http://feingold.org/research.shtml.

h. Abstract in PubMed database: S. Schoenthaler, et al, 1986, "The Impact of a Low Food Additive and Sucrose Diet on Academic Performance in 803 New York City Public Schools," *International Journal for Biosocial and Medical Research* Vol. 8 (2), pp. 18, e47, 5-195 [Internet, WWW], Available: The Fiengold Association of the United States; Address: http://feingold.org/research.shtml.

i. Abstract in PubMed database: J. Swanson and M. Kinsbourne, March 28, 1980, "Food Dyes Impair Performance of Hyperactive Children on a Laboratory Learning Test," *Science Magazine* Vol. 207, pp. 1485-1487 [Internet, WWW], Available: The Fiengold Association of the United States; Address: http://feingold.org/research.shtml.

57. Begley with Hager, p.57.

58.a. "Babies Learn Language Basics by Six Months," 1995, *The Sound Beginnings Newsletter* Vol. 1 (1) [Internet, WWW], Available: Sound Beginnings; Address: http://www.soundbeginnings.com.

b. Begley, *et al*, *Newsweek* February 19, 1996, p.57.

c. Polaneczky, pp. 102-106.

d. Lansdown and Walker, p. 135.

e. Geoffrey Cowley with Donna Foote, Special Edition Spring/ Summer 1997, "The Language Explosion," *Newsweek*, p. 23.

59. Ledson, pp. 50-52.

60.a. "Start Young to Get Your Head around Languages" *The Sound Beginnings Newsletter* Vol. 1 (1) [Internet, WWW], Available: Sound Beginnings; Address: http://www.soundbeginnings.com.

b. "Infants Can Detect Syllable Changes," 1995, *The Sound Beginnings Newsletter* Vol. 1 (1) [Internet, WWW], Available: Sound Beginnings; Address: http://www.soundbeginnings.com.

61.a. Begley with Hager, p. 62.

b. Claudia Kalb and Tessa Namuth, Special Edition Spring/ Summer 1997, "When a Child's Silence Isn't Golden," *Newsweek*, p. 23.

62. Patrick Kavanaugh, Ph.D., 1995, *Raising Musical Kids* (Ann Arbor, MI: Servant Publications), p. 21.

63.a. Begley with Hager, p. 57.

b. Mike, "Baby Brain Power."

64. Kavanaugh, p. 31.

65. "Music Lessons for Your Two-Year-Old?," February 22, 1980, *Awake!*, p. 26.

66. Kavanaugh.

67.a. J. M.. Flynn, M. H. Rahbar, and A. J. Bernstein, February 1996, "Is There an Association between Season of Birth and Reading Disability?," *Journal of Developmental and Behavioral Pediatrics* Vol. 17 (1), pp. 22-26.

b. Ledson 61-63.

68. I Am Your Child, Reiner Foundation, undated, "The First Years Last Forever," (Washington, DC: I Am Your Child), p. 6. Published brochure. Available from the author, [Internet, WWW], Address: http://www.iamyourchild.org.

69. Vicki Lansky, October 24, 1995, "Telling Stories to Your Child," *ParenTalk Newsletter* [Internet, WWW], Available: The National Parenting Center, Address: http://208.215.168.143/parentalk/toddlers/todd18.html.

70. Ledson, p. 68.

71. "Begin Teaching Your Baby to Read," September 22, 1982, *Awake!*, pp. 23-26.

72. Thomas Armstrong, Ph.D., October 24, 1995, "The Teach-Your-Baby-to-Read Movement," *ParenTalk Newsletter* [Internet, WWW], Available: The National Parenting Center, Address: http://208.215.168.143/parentalk/infancy/infant2.html.

73. Glen Doman, 1979, *Teach Your Baby Math*, (New York, NY: Simon and Schuster), p. 81.

74. Glen Doman, 1983, *How to Teach Your Baby to Read*, Second Edition, (Philadelphia, PA: Better Baby Press).

75. Doman, *Teach Your Baby Math.*

76. Burton L. White, 1995, *The New First Three Years of Life*, (New York, NY: Fireside Book).

77. Jacob.

78. Jerome L. Singer, "Imaginative Play and Adaptive Development," in Jeffrey S. Goldstein (ed.), 1994, *Toys, Play and Child Development* (New York, NY: Cambridge University Press), p. 18.

79. Jacob, p. 82.

80. "Mom, I Cannot Do It Without You," p. 7.

81. Ledson, pp. 54-55.

82. *Parents*' Child Development Toys, *Tracking Tube Play & Learning Guide*, "Providing the Right Tools for the Job," N9556A 8910 (USA:CNI), p. 8. Published brochure. Available from the author.

83. *Parents*' Child Development Toys, *Star Rings Play & Learning Guide*, "All Hear This! (Hearing and Infant Development," N9744A 8263 (USA:CNI), p. 11. Published brochure. Available from the author.

84. Bennett I. Berenthal and Joseph J. Campos, "A Systems Approach to the Organizing Effects of Self-Produced Locomotion during Infancy," in Carolyn Rovee-Collier and Lewis P. Lipsitt (eds.), 1990, *Advances in Infancy Research,* Volume 6 (Norwood, NJ: Ablex Publishing Corporation), pp. 21-25.

85.a. Lorie Parch, February 1998, "Walkers May Inhibit Walking," *Parenting's BabyTalk* Vol. 63 (1), p. 30.

b. Case Western Reserve University. January 22, 1998. "Study Puts Wheels on the Case Against the Baby Walker." [Internet, WWW]. Address: http://www.cwru.edu/pubaff/univcomm/babywalk.htm.

c. Carolyn Hagan, May 1998, "More Walker Woes," *Child*, pp. 41-43.

d. Karen Springen, June 23, 1997, "A Faltering First Step," *Newsweek*, p. 62.

e. Ledson, pp. 53-54.

86. Gail Kelso, M.S., August 1, 1995, "Evaluating Childcare." Photocopied flyer. Available from the author.

87. Randi Hutter Epstein, M.D., June 1999, "10 Ways to Prevent Postpartum Depression," *Parents* Vol. 74 (6), pp. 161-162.

88. Tiffany Field, Ph.D., November 1998, "Early Interventions for Infants of Depressed Mothers," *Pediatrics* Vol. 102 (5), p. 1308.

89. Epstein, p. 162.

90. Lisa Keller, OB-GYN, January 13, 1999, "Are Antidepressants Safe During Pregnancy?," *ParentTime* [Internet, WWW], Available: *Parenting's BabyTalk* website, Address: http://www.pathfinder.com/ParentTime/Ask/keller011399.html.

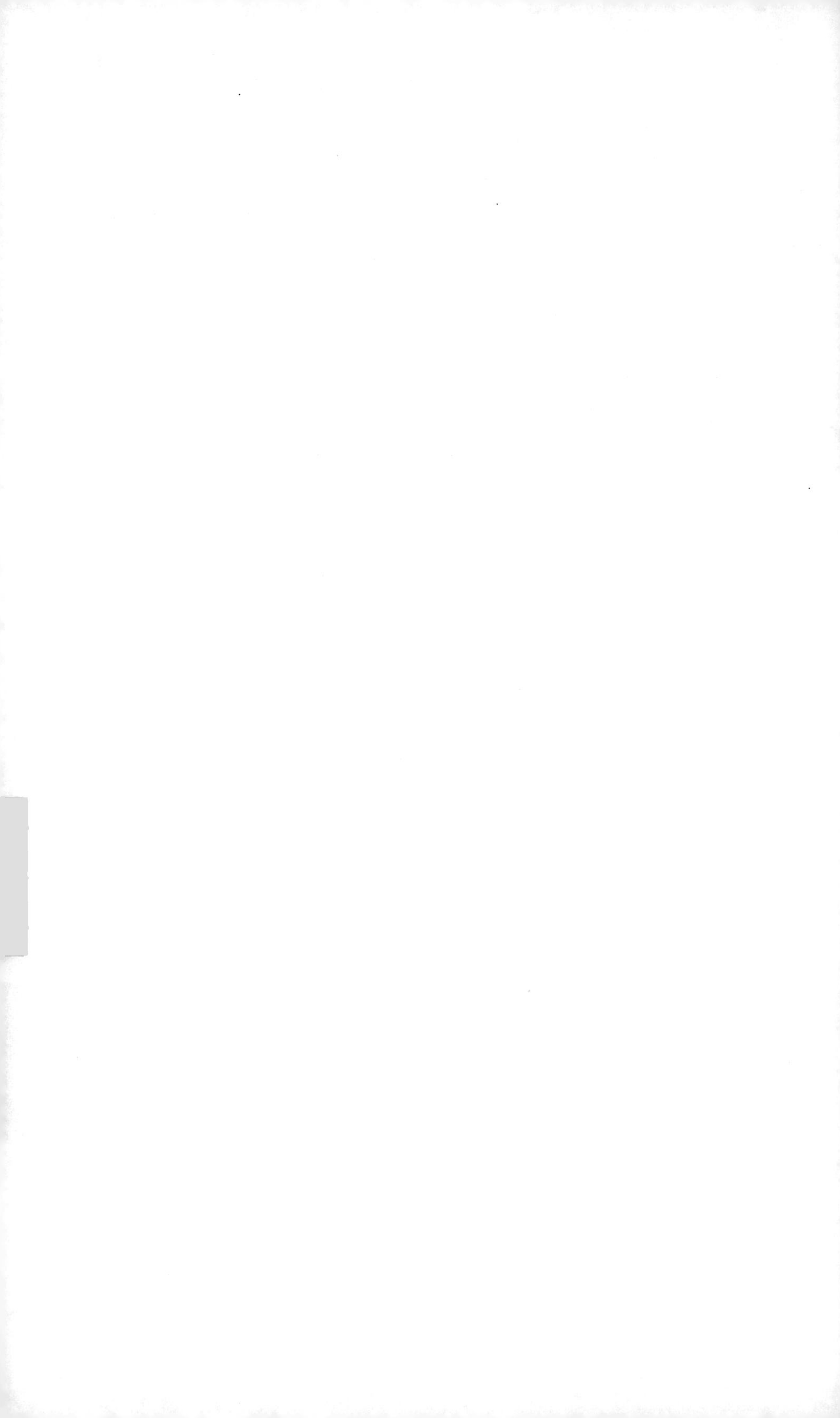

Bibliography

Bibliography

"101 Reasons to Breastfeed Your Child." 1998. [Internet, WWW]. Available: ProMoM, Inc.; Address: http://www.promom.org/101.

"ABC 'Prime Time Live' Explores Your Child's Brain." 1995. *The Sound Beginnings Newsletter* Vol. 1 (1). [Internet, WWW]. Available: Sound Beginnings, Address: http://www.soundbeginnings.com.

Abstract in *Pediatrics* database. Barros, F. C., C. G. Victora, T. C. Semer, S. Tonioli Filho, E. Tomasi, and E. Weiderpass. April 1995. "Use of Pacifiers Is Associated with Decreased Breastfeeding Duration." *Pediatrics* Vol. 95 (4), pp. 497-499. [Internet, WWW]. Available: American Academy of Pediatrics; Address: http://www.pediatrics.org.

Abstract in *Pediatrics* database. Niemela, M., M. Uhari, and M. Mottonen. November 1995. "A Pacifier Increases the Risk of Recurrent Acute Otitis Media in Children in Day Care Centers." *Pediatrics* Vol. 96 (5), pp. 884-888. [Internet, WWW]. Available: American Academy of Pediatrics; Address: http://www.pediatrics.org.

Abstract in *Pediatrics* database. Kate North, Peter Fleming, Jean Golding, and the ALSPAC Study Team. March 1999. "Pacifier Use and Morbidity in the First Six Months of Life." *Pediatrics* Vol. 103 (3), pp. E34. [Internet, WWW]. Available: American Academy of Pediatrics; Address: http://www.pediatrics.org.

Abstract in *Pediatrics* database. Victora, Cesar Gomes, Dominique Pareja Behague, Fernando Celso Barros, Maria Teresa Anselmo Olinto, and Elizabeth Weiderpass. March 1997. "Pacifier Use and Short Breastfeeding Duration: Cause, Consequence, or Coincidence?" *Pediatrics* Vol. 99 (3), pp. 445-453. [Internet, WWW]. Available: American Academy of Pediatrics; Address: http://www.pediatrics.org.

Abstract. In PubMed database. Boris, M. and F. Mandel. May 1994. "Foods and Additives Are Common Causes of the Attention Deficit Hyperactive Disorder in Children." *Annals of Allergy* Vol. 72, pp.462-468. [Internet, WWW]. Available: The

Fiengold Association of the United States; Address: http://feingoid.org/research.shtml.

Abstract. In PubMed database. Breakey, J. June 1997. "Review: The Role of Diet and Behaviour in Childhood." *Journal of Paediatric Child Health* Vol. 33 (3), pp. 190-194. [Internet, WWW]. Available: The Fiengold Association of the United States; Address: http://feingold.org/research.shtml.

Abstract in PubMed database. Dawson, G., K. Frey, H. Panagiotides, J. Osterling, and D. Hessl. February 1997. "Infants of Depressed Mothers Exhibit Atypical Frontal Brain Activity: A Replication and Extension of Previous Findings." *Journal of Child Psychology and Psychiatry* Vol. 38 (2), pp. 179-186. [Internet, WWW]. Available: PubMed Database; Address: http://www.ncbi.nlm.nih.gov.

Abstract in PubMed database. Dawson, G., H. Panagiotides, L. G. Klinger, and S. Spieker. July 1997. "Infants of Depressed and Nondepressed Mothers Exhibit Differences in Frontal Brain Electrical Activity during the Expression of Negative Emotions." *Developmental Psychology* Vol. 33 (4), pp. 650-656. [Internet, WWW]. Available: PubMed Database; Address: http://www.ncbi.nlm.nih.gov.

Abstract. In PubMed database. Nsouli, T. M., S. M. Nsouli, R. E. Linde, F. O'Mara, R. T. Scanlon, and J. A. Bellanti. September 1994. "Role of Food Allergy in Serious Otitis Media," *Annals of Allergy* Vol.73 (3), pp.215-219. [Internet, WWW]. Available: The Fiengold Association of the United States; Address: http://feingold.org.research.shtml.

Abstract. In PubMed database. Schoenthaler, S., et al. 1986. "The Impact of a Low Food Additive and Sucrose Diet on Academic Performance in 803 New York City Public Schools." *International Journal for Biosocial and Medical Research* Vol. 8 (2), pp. 18, e47, 5-195. [Internet, WWW]. Available: The Fiengold Association of the United States; Address: http://feingold.org/research.shtml.

Abstract. In PubMed database. Schoenthaler, S., J. Moody, and L. Pankow. November 1, 1991. "Applied Nutrition and Behavior," *Journal of Applied Nutrition* Vol. 43. [Internet, WWW]. Available: The Fiengold Association of the United States; Address: http://feingold.org/research.shtml.

Abstract. In PubMed database. Swanson, J. and M. Kinsbourne. March 28, 1980. "Food Dyes Impair Performance of Hyperactive Children on a Laboratory Learning Test." *Science Magazine* Vol. 207, pp. 1485-1487. [Internet, WWW]. Available: The Fiengold Association of the United States; Address: http://feingold.org/research.shtml.

Abstract in PubMed database. Yogman, M. W., D. Kindlon, and F. Earls. June 1996. "Father Involvement and Cognitive/ Behavioral Outcomes of Preterm Infants." *Journal of the American Academy of Child and Adolescent Psychiatry* Vol. 35 (6), pp. 699-700. [Internet, WWW]. Available: PubMed Database; Address: http://www.ncbi.nlm.nih.gov.

Adler, Jerry. Special Edition Spring/Summer 1997. "It's a Wise Father Who Knows . . ." *Newsweek*, p. 73.

"Are You Ready for Your Newcomer?" February 22, 1973. *Awake!*, pp. 16-19.

Armstrong, Thomas, Ph.D. October 24, 1995. "Awaken the Natural Genius in Your Kids." *ParenTalk Newsletter*. [Internet, WWW]. Available: The National Parenting Center, Address: http://208.215.168.143/parentalk/toddlers/todd27.html.

Armstrong, Thomas, Ph.D. October 24, 1995. "How Your Infant Learns." *ParenTalk Newsletter*. [Internet, WWW]. Available: The National Parenting Center, Address: http://www.tnpc.com.

Armstrong, Thomas, Ph.D. October 24, 1995. "How Your Toddler Learns." *ParenTalk Newsletter*. [Internet, WWW]. Available: The National Parenting Center, Address: http://www.tnpc.com/parentalk/toddlers.html.

Armstrong, Thomas, Ph.D. October 24, 1995. "The Teach-Your-Baby-to-Read Movement." *ParenTalk Newsletter*. [Internet, WWW]. Available: The National Parenting Center, Address: http://208.215.168.143/parentalk/infancy/infant2.html.

Associated Press. August 5, 1997. "Oh, That Cute Little Baaaaaby Talk." *Newsday*. [Internet, WWW]. Available: Electronic Library Fee-Based Service, Address: http:www.electroniclibrary.com. A copy of this article is available from the author.

"Babies and Toddlers at Greater Risk in Child Care." October 21, 1997. [Internet, WWW]. Available: Zero to Three; Address: http://www.zerotothree.org/baberisk.html.

"Babies Learn Language Basics by Six Months." 1995. *The Sound Beginnings Newsletter* Vol. 1 (1). [Internet, WWW]. Available: Sound Beginnings; Address: http://www.soundbeginnings.com.

Barr, Ronald G., M.A., M.D.C.M., F.R.C..P.(C.). "Reduction of Infant Crying by Parent Carrying." In Nina Gunzenhauser (ed.). 1990. *Advances in Touch: New Implications in Human Development*, Pediatric Round Table Series: 14. USA: Johnson & Johnson Consumer Products, Inc., pp. 105-113.

"Begin Teaching Your Baby to Read." September 22, 1982. *Awake!*, pp. 23-26.

Begley, Sharon and Pat Wingert. April 28, 1997. "Teach Your Parents Well." *Newsweek*, p. 72.

Begley, Sharon with Andrew Murr. Special Edition Spring/Summer 1997. "How to Build a Baby's Brain." *Newsweek*, pp. 28-32.

Begley, Sharon with Mary Hager. February 19, 1996. "Your Child's Brain." *Newsweek*, p. 54-62.

Bell, Allison. March 1999. "Let the Games Begin." *American Baby* Vol. LXI (3), pp. 38-43.

Berenthal, Bennett I. and Joseph J. Campos. "A Systems Approach to the Organizing Effects of Self-Produced Locomotion during Infancy." In Rovee-Collier, Carolyn and Lewis P. Lipsitt, (eds.). 1990. *Advances in Infancy Research,* Volume 6. Norwood, NJ: Ablex Publishing Corporation, pp. 1-60.

"Breastfeeding: The Best Start for Your Baby." December 1997. LF808 (Evansville, IN: Mead Johnson & Company). Published brochure. Available from the author.

"Breast Feeding — A Mother's Loving 'Sacrifice'." June 8, 1983. *Awake!*, pp. 20-22.

"Breast-Feeding Basics." August 22, 1994. *Awake!*, pp. 10-13.

Brott, Armin with additional reporting by Nina Martin. September 1997. "Born to Be Wild . . . or Mild?" *Parenting's BabyTalk* Vol. 62 (7), pp. 32-39.

Brott, Armin with additional reporting by Laura D'Angelo. June/July 1997. "What a Difference a Dad Makes." *Parenting's BabyTalk* Vol. 62 (5), pp. 32-39.

Brown, J. Larry Ph.D., and Lori P. Marcotte, M.S., M.P.H., R.D. January/February 1999. "Nutrition and Cognitive Development in Children." *Early Childhood News.* [Internet, WWW].

Available: *Early Childhood News*; Address: http://www.earlychildhoodnews.com/archive/nutri.htm.

Case Western Reserve University. January 22, 1998. "Study Puts Wheels on the Case Against the Baby Walker." [Internet, WWW]. Address: http://www.cwru.edu/pubaff/univcomm/babywalk.htm.

"Collected Net Articles of Dr. Kalle Reichelt." [Internet, WWW]. Address: http://www.panix.com/~donwiss/reichelt.html.

Committee on Nutrition, 1991 to 1992. Part 1 June 1992. "The Use of Whole Cow's Milk in Infancy (RE925 1)." *Pediatrics* Vol. 89 (6), pp. 1105-1109. [Internet, WWW]. Available: American Academy of Pediatrics; Address: http://www.aap.org/policy/04788.html.

Committee on Sports Medicine, 1986-1988. November 1988. "Infant Exercise Programs (RE8132)." *Pediatrics* Vol. 82 (5), p. 800. [Internet, WWW]. Available: American Academy of Pediatrics; Address: http://www.aap.org/policy/02223.html.

Committee on Sports Medicine, 1984-1985. April 1985 (reaffirmed February 1990). "Infant Swimming Programs (RE5045)." *Pediatrics* Vol. 75 (4). [Internet, WWW]. Available: American Academy of Pediatrics; Address: http://www.aap.org/policy/362.html.

Cowley, Geoffrey with Donna Foote. Special Edition Spring/Summer 1997. "The Language Explosion." *Newsweek*, p. 23.

Crook, William G., M.D. 1986. *The Yeast Connection*. New York: NY: Random House.

Cunningham, Allan S., M.D. "Nutrition in the First Year." In Nicholas Cunningham, M.D., Dr. P.H., Donald F. Tapley, M.D., Genell J. Subak-Sharpe, M.S., and Diane M. Goetz (eds.). 1990. *The Columbia University College of Physicians and Surgeons Complete Guide to Early Childcare*. New York, NY: Crown Publishers, Inc., pp. 32-44.

Cunningham, Nicholas, M.D., Dr. P.H. "Caring for the Newborn." In Nicholas Cunningham, M.D., Dr. P.H., Donald F. Tapley, M.D., Genell J. Subak-Sharpe, M.S., and Diane M. Goetz (eds.). 1990. *The Columbia University College of Physicians and Surgeons Complete Guide to Early Childcare*. New York, NY: Crown Publishers, Inc., p. 11-24.

Dawson, Geraldine, David Hessl, and Karin Frey. 1994. "Social Influences on Early Developing Biological and Behavioral Systems Related to Risk for Affective Disorder." *Development and Psychopathology* Vol. 6, pp. 759-779. Summarized in "The Effect of Maternal Depression on Infant/Toddler Emotional Development." 1997. *Supplement to Module III Materials, The Program for Infant/Toddler Caregivers.* Unpublished Manuscript. [Internet, WWW]. Available: Early Head Start National Resource Center; Address: http://www.ehsnrc.org/rmdepre.htm.

Doman Glen and Janet Doman. 1994. *How to Teach Your Baby to Read.* Garden City Park, NY: Avery Publishing Group.

Doman, Glen. 1979. *Teach Your Baby Math.* New York, NY: Simon and Schuster.

Ebrahim, Professor G. J. and Dr. William Cutting. 4th Quarter 1998. "Update on Breastfeeding." *Child Health Dialogue* Issue 9. [Internet, WWW]. Available: World Health Organization; Address: http://www.who.int/chd/pub/newslet/dialog/9/update_on_breastfeeding.htm.

Eden, Alvin, M.D. October 24, 1995. "Toddler Exercises." *ParenTalk Newsletter.* [Internet, WWW]. Available: The National Parenting Center, Address: http://www.tnpc.com.

Epstein, Randi Hutter, M.D. June 1999. "10 Ways to Prevent Postpartum Depression." *Parents* Vol. 74 (6), pp. 161-162.

Erickson, Candace, M.D. "Emotional and Intellectual Development." In Nicholas Cunningham, M.D., Dr. P.H., Donald F. Tapley, M.D., Genell J. Subak-Sharpe, M.S., and Diane M. Goetz (eds.). 1990. *The Columbia University College of Physicians and Surgeons Complete Guide to Early Childcare.* New York, NY: Crown Publishers, Inc., pp. 147-156.

Evans, Laurie, M.A. "Impact of Infant Massage on the Neonate and the Parent-Infant Relationship." In Nina Gunzenhauser (ed.). 1990. *Advances in Touch: New Implications in Human Development*, Pediatric Round Table Series: 14. USA: Johnson & Johnson Consumer Products, Inc., pp. 71-80.

"Family Communication — How Can It Be Improved?" January 8, 1985. *Awake!*, pp. 4-10.

Field, Tiffany M., Ph.D. November 1998. "Early Interventions for Infants of Depressed Mothers." *Pediatrics* Vol. 102 (5), p. 1308.

Field, Tiffany M., Ph.D., and Saul M. Schanberg, M.D. "Massage Alters Growth and Catecholamine Production in Preterm Newborns." In Nina Gunzenhauser (ed.). 1990. *Advances in Touch: New Implications in Human Development*, Pediatric Round Table Series: 14. USA: Johnson & Johnson Consumer Products, Inc., pp. 96-104.

Flynn, J. M., M. H. Rahbar, and A. J. Bernstein. February 1996. "Is There an Association between Season of Birth and Reading Disability?" *Journal of Developmental and Behavioral Pediatrics* Vol. 17 (1), pp. 22-26.

Foulke, Judith E. September 1994. "Mercury in Fish: Cause for Concern?" *FDA Consumer*. [Internet, WWW]. Available: U.S. Food and Drug Administration, Address: http://vm.cfsan.fda.gov/~dms.

Freinkel, Susan. August 1997. "All about Ears." *Parenting's BabyTalk* Vol. 62 (6), pp. 34-37.

Friedman, Jenny, Ph.D. January 1998. "Genius?" *American Baby* Vol. LX (1), pp. 58-66.

"From the Cradle to the Grave, Our Greatest Need Is Love." September 22, 1986. *Awake!*, p. 4.

Gewirtz, Jacob L., Ph.D., and Albert R. Hollenbeck, Ph.D. "Effects on Parents of Contact/Touch in the Postpartum Hour." In Nina Gunzenhauser (ed.). 1990. *Advances in Touch: New Implications in Human Development*, Pediatric Round Table Series: 14. USA: Johnson & Johnson Consumer Products, Inc., pp. 62-71.

Gilbert, Sue, M.S. 1999. "Fish Safety Concerns." ParentsPlace.com. [Internet, WWW]. Available:ParentsPlace.com, Address: http://www.parentsplace.com/expert/nutritionist/safety/qa/0,348 8,1 2042,00.html.

Glick, Daniel. Special Edition Spring/Summer 1997. "Rooting for Intelligence." *Newsweek*, p. 32.

Greenough, William, Ph.D., Harry Chugani, M.D., and Craig Ramey, Ph.D. October 4, 1994. Interview by Michelle Trudeau, "Enriched Environments Positively Affect Intelligence." *All Things Considered*. National Public Radio. [Internet, WWW]. Available: Electronic Library Fee-Based Service; Address: http://www.electroniclibrary.com. A copy of this article is available from the author.

Gullen, Michael, Ph.D. and Joan Lunden. April 4, 1997. "Parenting: The First Years Last Forever." *Good Morning America.* American Broadcasting Companies, Inc. [Internet, WWW]. Available: Electronic Library Fee-Based Service; Address: http://www.electroniclibrary.com. A copy of this transcript is available from the author.

Hagan, Carolyn. May 1998. "More Walker Woes." *Child*, pp. 41-43.

Horwood, L. John and David M. Fergusson. January 1998. "Breastfeeding and Later Cognitive and Academic Outcomes." *Pediatrics* Vol. 101 (1). [Internet, WWW]. Available: American Academy of Pediatrics; Address: http://www.pediatrics.org/cgi/content/full/101/1/e9.

"How Your Baby Learns Language." September 1995. *American Baby*. Reprinted in *The Sound Beginnings Newsletter* Vol. 1 (2). [Internet, WWW]. Available: Sound Beginnings; Address: http://www.soundbeginnings.com.

Howard, Cynthia R., Fred M. Howard, Bruce Lanphear, Elisabeth A. DeBlieck, Shirley Eberly, and Ruth A. Lawrence. March 1999. "The Effects of Early Pacifier Use on Breastfeeding Duration." *Pediatrics* Vol. 103 (3) p. e33. [Internet, WWW]. Available: American Academy of Pediatrics; Address: http://www.pediatrics.org/cgi/content/full/103/3/e33.

I Am Your Child, Reiner Foundation. Undated. "The First Years Last Forever." Washington, DC: I Am Your Child. Published brochure. Available from the author. [Internet, WWW]. Address: http://www.iamyourchild.org.

"Infants Can Detect Syllable Changes." 1995. *The Sound Beginnings Newsletter* Vol. 1 (1). [Internet, WWW]. Available: Sound Beginnings; Address: http://www.soundbeginnings.com.

Jacob, S. H., Ph.D. 1991. *Your Baby's Mind.* Holbrook, MA: Bob Adams, Inc.

"Johnny, Please Be Quiet!" September 8, 1982. *Awake!*, pp. 16-20.

Kalb, Claudia and Tessa Namuth. Special Edition Spring/Summer 1997. "When a Child's Silence Isn't Golden." *Newsweek*, p. 23.

Kantrowitz, Barbara. Special Edition Spring/Summer 1997. "Off to a Good Start." *Newsweek*, pp. 6-9.

Kavanaugh, Patrick, Ph.D. 1995. *Raising Musical Kids.* Ann Arbor, MI: Servant Publications.

Keller, Lisa, OB-GYN. January 13, 1999. "Are Antidepressants Safe During Pregnancy?" *ParentTime* [Internet, WWW]. Available:

Parenting's BabyTalk website, Address: http://www.pathfinder.com/ParentTime/Ask/keller011399.html.

Kelso, Gail, M.S. August 1, 1995. "Evaluating Childcare." Photocopied flyer. Available from the author.

Kennell, John H., M.D. "Doula-Mother and Parent-Infant Contact." In Nina Gunzenhauser (ed.). 1990. *Advances in Touch: New Implications in Human Development*, Pediatric Round Table Series: 14. USA: Johnson & Johnson Consumer Products, Inc., pp. 53-62.

Landers, Cassie, Ed.D., M.P.H. "Child-Rearing Practices and Infant Development in South India." In Nina Gunzenhauser (ed.). 1990. *Advances in Touch: New Implications in Human Development*, Pediatric Round Table Series: 14. USA: Johnson & Johnson Consumer Products, Inc., pp. 42-53.

Lansdown, Richard and Marjorie Walker. 1991. *Your Child's Development from Birth through Adolescence*. New York, NY: Alfred A. Knopf, Inc.

Lansky, Vicky. October 24, 1995. "Telling Stories to Your Child." *ParenTalk Newsletter*. [Internet, WWW]. Available: The National Parenting Center, Address: http://208.215.168.143/parentalk/toddlers/todd18.html.

Layton, Richard E., M.D. 1998. "Patient of the Month: Marshall." [Internet, WWW]. Available: Allergy Connection, Address: http://www.allergyconnection.com/PATIENT/marshall.html.

"Learning Begins in the Womb." January 22, 1992. *Awake!*, p. 14-17.

"Learning 'from Infancy.'" April 8, 1982. *Awake!*, p. 15.

"Learning Language — The Younger, The Better, So Why Do Schools Delay?" 1995. *The Sound Beginnings Newsletter* Vol. 1 (4). [Internet, WWW]. Available: Sound Beginnings, Address: http://www.soundbeginnings.com.

Ledson, Sidney. 1987. *Raising Brighter Children: A Program for Busy Parents*. New York, NY: Walker and Company.

Levy, Gary, Ph.D. August 1997. "The Wonder Year: Vanishing Act." *Parenting's BabyTalk* Vol. 62 (7), pp. 19-20.

Levy, Gary, Ph.D. September 1997. "The Wonder Year: Basic Instincts." *Parenting's BabyTalk* Vol. 62 (7), pp. 17-19.

Lipsitt, Lewis P., Ph.D. November 5, 1998. "Learning and Emotion in Infants." *Pediatrics* Vol. 102 (5), pp.1262-1267.

"Love at First Sight — And Forever After!" September 22, 1991. *Awake!*, pp. 5-9.

McCalley, Dee. "Any Child Can Become Multilingual." 1995. *The Sound Beginnings Newsletter* Vol. 1 (3). [Internet, WWW]. Available: Sound Beginnings; Address: http://www.soundbeginnings.com.

Meaney, Michael J., Ph.D., David H. Aitken, M.Sc., Seema Bhatnagar, M.Sc., Shari R. Bodnoff, M.A., John B. Mitchell, Ph.D., and Alain Sarrieau, Ph.D. "Neonatal Handling and the Development of the Adrenocortical Response to Stress." In Nina Gunzenhaúser (ed.). 1990. *Advances in Touch: New Implications in Human Development*, Pediatric Round Table Series: 14. USA: Johnson & Johnson Consumer Products, Inc., pp. 11-22.

"Media Alert: AAP Reaffirms Breastfeeding Stance Following Fictional TV Show." 1999. American Academy of Pediatrics. [Internet, WWW]. Available: American Academy of Pediatrics; Address: http://www.aap.org/visit/brmdalt.htm.

Merriman, Anne. February 1998. "A Touching Development." *Parenting's BabyTalk* Vol. 63 (1), p. 29.

Michels, Dia L. April 1998. "Breastfeeding Is Best Feeding." *Parenting's BabyTalk*, Vol. 63 (3), p. 21.

Mike, John, M.D. 1999. "Baby Brain Power Expanding the Mind Prenatally." *Childbirth Instructor Magazine*. [Internet, WWW]. Available: Brilliant Babies Powerful Adults, John Mike, M.D., Address: http://www.smart-baby.com/article-1.htm.

Miles, Karen. September 1997. "Vision Quest." *Parenting's BabyTalk* Vol. 62 (7), pp. 57-60.

"Mom, I Cannot Do without You." August 22, 1977. *Awake!*, pp. 6-8.

"'Motherese' Helps Babies Learn from Their Parents." 1995. *The Sound Beginnings Newsletter* Vol. 1 (1). [Internet, WWW]. Available: Sound Beginnings, Address: http://www.soundbeginnings.com.

"Music Lessons for Your Two-Year-Old?" February 22, 1980. *Awake!*, p. 25-28.

Nash, J. Madeline. February 3, 1997. "Special Report: Fertile Minds." *Time* Vol. 149 (5), p. 48-56.

Ochshorn, Susan. Undated. "How Smart Is Your Baby?" *Parenting* [Internet, WWW]. Available: *Parenting's BabyTalk* website, Address: http://www.pathfinder.com/ParentTime/Growing/smartba.html?az.

Olinwenstein, Lori. April 1999. "What Parents Need to Know about Nutrition." *Parenting's BabyTalk* Vol. 64 (3), pp. 22-23.

"Pacifiers Linked to a Decrease in Breastfeeding." March 1, 1999. Press Release. [Internet,WWW]. Available: American Academy of Pediatrics; Address: http://www.pediatrics.org.

Parch, Lorie. February 1998. "Walkers May Inhibit Walking." *Parenting's BabyTalk* Vol. 63 (1), p. 30.

Parents' Child Development Toys, *Balls in a Bowl Play & Learning Guide*. "Intelligence: All Kinds of Smart." N9562A 8363. USA: CNI. Published brochure. Available from the author.

Parents' Child Development Toys, *Balls in a Bowl Play & Learning Guide*. "On the Go." N9562A 8363. USA: CNI. Published brochure. Available from the author.

Parents' Child Development Toys, *Stack and Fit Play & Learning Guide*. "Team Play Means Twice the Fun." N9595A 8124. USA: CNI. Published brochure. Available from the author.

Parents' Child Development Toys, *Fitting Forms Play & Learning Guide*. "One + One = Fun (Early Math)." N9564A 8331. USA: CNI. Published brochure. Available from the author.

Parents' Child Development Toys, *Red Rings Play & Learning Guide*. "Reaching for the Rings." RRN9554A 8622. USA: CNI. Published brochure. Available from the author.

Parents' Child Development Toys, *Red Rings Play & Learning Guide*. "Solitary Play: Learning to Amuse Yourself." RRN9554A 8622. USA: CNI. Published brochure. Available from the author.

Parents' Child Development Toys, *Rhythm Rollers Play & Learning Guide*. "Playing with the Big Kids." 8262. USA: Atlas Editions. Published brochure. Available from the author.

Parents' Child Development Toys, *Stack and Fit Play & Learning Guide*. "Team Play Means Twice the Fun." N9595A 8124. USA: CNI. Published brochure. Available from the author.

Parents' Child Development Toys, *Stack and Fit Play & Learning Guide*. "The Formation of Concepts." N9595A 8124. USA: CNI. Published brochure. Available from the author.

Parents' Child Development Toys, *Star Rings Play & Learning Guide*. "All Hear This! (Hearing and Infant Development." N9744A 8263. USA: CNI. Published brochure. Available from the author.

Parents' Child Development Toys, *Star Rings Play & Learning Guide.* "Would You Like to Swing on a Star?" N9744A 8263. USA: CNI. Published brochure. Available from the author.

Parents' Child Development Toys, *Tracking Tube Play & Learning Guide.* "Providing the Right Tools for the Job." N9556A 8910. USA: CNI. Published brochure. Available from the author.

Parents' Child Development Toys, *Visual Display Play & Learning Guide.* "Intellectual and Social Skills." N9521A 8914. USA: CNI. Published brochure. Available from the author.

Parents' Child Development Toys, *Visual Display Play & Learning Guide.* "The Story Behind the Smile." N9521A 8914. USA: CNI. Published brochure. Available from the author.

"People — Why They Act the Way They Do." April 8, 1980. *Awake!*, pp. 8-11.

Polaneczky, Ronnie. March 1, 1998. "How Kids Get Smart: The Surprising News." *Redbook* Vol. 190, pp. 102-106. [Internet, WWW]. Available: Electronic Library Fee-Based Service; Address: http://www.electroniclibrary.com. A copy of this article is available from the author.

Popenoe, David. March 1, 1996. "A World without Fathers (Consequences of Children Living without Fathers)." *The Wilson Quarterly* Vol. 20, pp. 12-18. [Internet, WWW]. Available: Electronic Library Fee-Based Service; Address: http://www.electroniclibrary.com. A copy of this article is available from the author.

Reite, Martin, M.D. "Effects of Touch on the Immune System." In Nina Gunzenhauser (ed.). 1990. *Advances in Touch: New Implications in Human Development*, Pediatric Round Table Series: 14. USA: Johnson & Johnson Consumer Products, Inc., pp. 22-31.

"Research on Fatherhood — Old Discoveries Seem New Again." Undated. [Internet, WWW]. Available: Men's Health Network, Address: http://menshealthnetwork.org/library/mhndocs/ Fatherhd.html.

Schanberg, Saul M., M.D., Cynthia M. Kuhn, Ph.D., Tiffany M. Field, Ph.D., and Jorge V. Bartolome, Ph.D. "Maternal Deprivation and Growth Suppression." In Nina Gunzenhauser (ed.). 1990. *Advances in Touch: New Implications in Human Development*, Pediatric Round Table Series: 14. USA: Johnson & Johnson Consumer Products, Inc., pp. 3-10.

Sears, William, M.D., and Martha Sears, R.N. Undated. "Early Walkers, Late Walkers." *ParentTime* [Internet, WWW]. Available: *Parenting's BabyTalk* website, Address: http://www.pathfinder.com/ParentTime/sears/leafs/earlywk.html.

Sears, William, M.D. April 1999. "Smart from the Start." *Parenting's BabyTalk* Vol. 64 (3), pp. 24-28.

Sears, William, M.D. *The Baby Book.* Special excerpt reprinted by NoJo, Inc. 1992. "BabyWearing: An Introduction to The Original Babysling."

Sethi, Anita, Ph.D. April 1999. "Mother Tongue." *Parenting's BabyTalk* Vol. 64 (3), pp.17-18.

Shogren, Elizabeth. April 18, 1997. "White House 'Baby Talk' Raises Child Care's Significance." Home Edition, *Los Angeles Times*, p. A-21. [Internet, WWW]. Available: Electronic Library Fee-Based Service; Available: http://www.electroniclibrary.com. A copy of this article is available from the author.

Singer, Jerome L. "Imaginative Play and Adaptive Development." In Goldstein, Jeffrey S. (ed.). 1994. *Toys, Play and Child Development.* New York, NY: Cambridge University Press, pp. 6-26.

Springen, Karen. June 23, 1997. "A Faltering First Step." *Newsweek*, p. 62.

"Start Young to Get Your Head around Languages." 1995. *The Sound Beginnings Newsletter* Vol. 1 (1). [Internet, WWW]. Available: Sound Beginnings; Address: http://www.soundbeginnings.com.

Staso, William, Ph.D. "What Stimulation Your Baby Needs to Become Smart." [Internet, WWW]. Available: Great Beginnings Press, Address: http://www.utech.net/gbpress/book1005/smartinfo.htm.

Staso, William, Ph.D. December 1997. "'Windows of Opportunity' for Infants and Toddlers." [Internet, WWW]. Available: Great Beginnings Press, Address: http://www.utech.net/gbpress/book1005/windowsop.htm.

Summers, Shannon. September 1998. "The Right Touch." *Parenting's BabyTalk* Vol. 63 (7), pp. 54-57.

"The BT Guide: First Foods." August 1997. *Parenting's BabyTalk* Vol. 62 (6), pp. 29-32.

"The Formative Years — What You Sow Now You Will Reap Later." September 22, 1992. *Awake!*, pp. 6-10.

The K.I.T. — The Kid's Intellectual Trainer. 1995. Los Angeles, CA: Wiz Kid Makers.

"Those Awesome Baby Brains!" May 22, 1987. *Awake!*, pp. 3-4.

"Train Your Child in the Right Way — And Do It from Infancy!" May 22, 1987. *Awake!*, pp. 7-11.

Underwood, Anne and Peter Plagens. Special Edition Spring/Summer 1997. "Little Artists and Athletes." *Newsweek*, pp. 14-15.

Van Boven, Sarah. Special Edition Spring/Summer 1997. "Giving Infants a Helping Hand." *Newsweek*, p. 45.

Vartabedian, Bryan S., M.D. April 1999. "Feed Me, Mommy." *American Baby* Vol. LXI (4), pp. 62-67.

Ward, Elizabeth, M.S., R.D. April 1999, "Smart Foods." *American Baby* Vol. LXI (4), p. 12.

Weber, Linda. May 1998. "Language Lessons." *Parenting's BabyTalk* Vol. 63 (4), pp. 35-39.

Weber, Linda. September 1997. "Ready to Wear." *Parenting's BabyTalk* Vol. 62 (7), pp. 48-54.

White, Burton L. 1995. *The New First Three Years of Life*. New York, NY: Fireside Book.

Wingate, Carrie, Ph.D. March 1999. "Look Who's Talking." *American Baby* Vol. LXI (3), pp. 8-13.

Wingert, Pat and Anne Underwood. Special Edition Spring/Summer 1997. "Hey — Look Out, World, Here I Come." *Newsweek*, pp. 12-15.

Work Group on Breastfeeding, 1996 to 1997. December 1997. "Breastfeeding and the Use of Human Milk (RE9729)." *Pediatrics* Vol. 100 (6), pp. 1035-1039. [Internet, WWW]. Available: American Academy of Pediatrics; Address: http://www.aap.org/policy/re9729.html.

World Health Organization. "The International Code of Marketing of Breastmilk Substitutes." The International Baby Food Action Network. [Internet, WWW]. Address: http://www.gn.apc.org/ibfan/fullcode.html.

"Why Breast-feeding Is Best Feeding." July 22, 1981. *Awake!*, pp. 21-23.

"You Can Boost Your Child's Brain Power." 1995. *The Sound Beginnings Newsletter* Vol. 1 (1). [Internet, WWW]. Available: Sound Beginnings, Address: http://www.soundbeginnings.com.

"Your Child's Growth: Developmental Milestones." 1999. Published brochure. [Internet, WWW]. Available: American Academy of Pediatrics; Address: http://www.aap.org/family/devmile.htm.

Index

Index